A Casebook of Psychoth Practice with Challengin

Most contemporary psychoanalysts and psychotherapists see each patient once or twice a week at most. As many patients have reached a marked state of distress before seeking treatment, this gives the analyst a difficult task to accomplish in what is a limited amount of time. *A Casebook of Psychotherapy Practice with Challenging Patients: A modern Kleinian approach* sets out a model for working with quite significantly disturbed, distressed, or resistant patients in a very limited time, which Robert Waska has termed "Modern Kleinian Therapy."

Each chapter provides a vivid look into the moment-to-moment workings of a contemporary Kleinian focus on understanding projective identification, enactment, and acting out as well as the careful and thoughtful interpretive work necessary in these complex clinical situations. Individual psychotherapeutic work is represented throughout the book alongside instructive reports of psychoanalytic work with disturbed couples, and the more challenging patient is illustrated with several comprehensive reviews of films that follow such hard-to-reach individuals.

A Casebook of Psychotherapy Practice with Challenging Patients: A modern Kleinian approach is filled with a combination of contemporary theory building, a wealth of clinical vignettes, and practical advice. It is a hands-on guide for psychoanalysts and therapists who need to get to grips with complex psychoanalytic concepts in a short time and shows the therapeutic power the Modern Kleinian Therapy approach can have and how it can enable them to work most effectively with difficult patients.

Robert Waska LPCC, MFT, PhD is an analytic member at the San Francisco Center for Psychoanalysis and conducts a full-time private psychoanalytic practice for individuals and couples in San Francisco and Marin County, California. He is the author of thirteen published textbooks on Kleinian psychoanalytic theory and technique, is a contributing author for three psychology texts, and has published over a hundred articles in professional journals.

A Casebook of Psychotherapy Practice with Challenging Patients

A modern Kleinian approach

Robert Waska

Routledge
Taylor & Francis Group

LONDON AND NEW YORK

First published 2015
by Routledge
27 Church Road, Hove, East Sussex, BN3 2FA

and by Routledge
711 Third Avenue, New York, NY 10017

Routledge is an imprint of the Taylor & Francis Group, an informa business

British Library Cataloguing in Publication Data
A catalogue record for this book is available from the British
Library

Library of Congress Cataloging in Publication Data
Waska, Robert T., author.
A casebook of psychotherapy practice with challenging patients :
a modern Kleinian approach / Robert Waska.
 p. ; cm.
 Includes bibliographical references and index.
 I. Title.
 [DNLM: 1. Klein, Melanie. 2. Psychoanalytic Therapy–methods–
 Case Reports. 3. Psychoanalytic Theory–Case Reports.
 WM 460.6]
 RC480
 616.89'14–dc23   2014033672

ISBN: 978-1-138-82005-0 (hbk)
ISBN: 978-1-138-82006-7 (pbk)
ISBN: 978-1-315-74400-1 (ebk)

Typeset in Times New Roman
By Wearset Ltd, Boldon, Tyne and Wear

MIX
Paper from
responsible sources
FSC   FSC® C013056
www.fsc.org

Printed and bound in Great Britain by
TJ International Ltd, Padstow, Cornwall

Contents

Acknowledgments

I wish to thank the patients I work with. They have afforded me the opportunity to be introduced to the particular issues examined in this book and the chance to use the analytic method to understand and change those struggles. The process of being an analyst is one in which the ability to understand and help is always being enriched by the next individual or couple one sees. Therefore, I am grateful to have the chance to visit these private and painful places my patients have endured and to help them seek psychic solutions. All identities have been disguised to protect the confidentiality of each case.

In addition, I am always thankful to my wife of some thirty years for her support and faith in my writing. In my day-to-day life, in my week-to-week clinical work, and in my ongoing writing career, she stands as a strong and faithful believer in what I do and what I strive towards. I thank Liz for being who she is.

I wish to thank the online journal Otherwise for permission to reprint the material in Chapter 1, and Fort Da for permission to reprint the material in Chapter 2. These chapters were previously published as Waska, R. (2012) Seven Sessions. In Modern Kleinian Therapy and One Patient's Somatic Retreat from Unbearable Loss, Other/Wise, the Online Journal of the International Forum for Psychoanalytic Education, Winter, Vol. 9; and Waska, R. (2013) Working with Psychotic Process: Noticing the Counter-Transference and Transference Dynamic in Early Analytic Treatment, Fort Da.

Introduction

In Chapter 1, case material is used to explore the somatic experience as a psychic battleground for conflicts regarding loss. The case report follows one patient who has been seen in psychoanalytic therapy from a Kleinian perspective for seven sessions so far. Details of the patient's struggle with loss and the resulting loyalty to a somatic retreat are examined. Projective identification, counter-transference, containment, and issues of enactment are discussed.

In addition, the author considers the technical elements of the analytic situation. In psychoanalytic treatment there is always an immediate transference process triggered the moment a treatment begins. With some patients this appears to be hidden, with no noticeable counter-transference impression. It may take time for the more obvious aspects of the transference to emerge. With other patients we can find and engage the various cords of unconscious phantasy being played out in the treatment setting from the very start. These elements are discussed in light of this very new and unfolding psychoanalytic narrative.

In Chapter 2, the author reports on the first two months of analytic treatment with a disturbed patient crippled with the anxieties of psychotic conflict. The elements of transference and counter-transference were vital in beginning to understand his internal phantasy state and psychological perspective. Clinical issues of containment, projective identification, and the dread of/despair for attachment to the object are explored from a Kleinian approach. Again, this is a very fresh analytic encounter but one in which Modern Kleinian Therapy establishes a very vital and immediate difference.

In Chapter 3, two cases of analytic treatment are provided to detail the traumatic struggles our patients encounter in traversing the depressive position and its particular anxieties. The case material illustrates the use of counter-transference as a tool in better understanding the patient's unconscious struggles with depressive phantasies (Klein 1935, 1940).

In the transference, both patients engaged the analyst in such a manner as to communicate, defend, deflect and deny their depressive phantasies regarding the desire for more from the object. This desire was followed by fears of what could happen to the object as a result. Projective identification was a significant element of the transference dynamic, creating a pull on the analyst to become part of the self–object conflict and to either take on certain restrictive and rigid roles or to be prevented from having other more independent or spontaneous capacities. In other words, give-and-take relating was often replaced with a conviction of demand and disappointment or desperate yearning and permanent loss.

In Chapter 4, the author uses two turbulent and brief case reports of hard-to-reach disturbed patients to demonstrate the intensity that may occur in the counter-transference. This state must be continuously managed and utilized rather than simply acted out. In our psychoanalytic practices, we encounter many borderline and narcissistic patients who are reluctant to establish any real emotional connection or exchange. As a result, we struggle with numerous jarring interactions in which we may only see a person one, two, or three times before there is a sudden collapse of any reciprocal engagement. It is not unusual in these psychological collisions for the patient to leave before ever starting a real treatment process. As a result of intense paranoid-schizoid (Klein 1946) fears and desires, it is common for such patients to abort the analytic contact (Waska 2007) as soon as it begins or to abruptly terminate after only a few chaotic sessions. The analyst is pushed to the limits in the counter-transference with these patients. Therefore, it is crucial to monitor the degree of enactment taking place and the depth of one's immersion within the patient's pathological projective identification patterns.

Chapter 5 examines the challenges of this counter-transference immersion. To be fully helpful, in a way that respects both the internal and external needs and conflicts of our patients in analytic treatment, we must become immersed in their emotional perspective so as to have a feel for how they view and value themselves and their objects. Allowing ourselves to be carried into their inner phantasies and to be in touch with their strivings towards and away from love, hate, and knowledge is important in the analytic process. Counter-transference is unavoidable; but, if properly monitored and contained, it can provide a beneficial therapeutic device.

However, when treating disturbed patients who draw us into more paranoid transference states or primitive depressive position conflicts, we are often involved in various degrees of enactment. Even then, the counter-transference, if carefully studied, can help us rebalance ourselves therapeutically and start to better understand how patients are using us in their internal world and why they need or desire to organize their object-relational world in such terms. We cannot help but be immersed within the patient's unconscious belief system. But, by being aware of our thoughts, feelings, and reactions, we can keep our head above the choppy counter-transference waters enough to act out less and offer constant interpretations that are more informed and focused on the patient's unique and personal object-relational conflicts and internal belief system.

In Chapter 6, three cases are examined in which loss of the maternal object by emotional absence or by death left the individual with lifelong phantasies and anxieties regarding the nature of self in relationship to the object and underlying feelings of emptiness and despair. All three patients had a chronic lack of control, confidence, or identity. Each had unique defensive methods of avoiding their core unconscious relational conflicts regarding love, hate, and desires to be understood and to understand others. Yet, there were certain similarities in how each patient tried to enlist the analyst to enact certain roles that either repeated and/or finally fulfilled specific underlying belief systems (Britton 1998) imbedded in their pathological organization (Rosenfeld 1983, 1987; Steiner 1990, 1993). This chapter explores the counter-transference experiences with each patent and the specific projective identification dynamics (Waska 2002, 2004) that shaped the transference and counter-transference profile.

Chapter 7 reviews the Modern Kleinian Therapy approach, examines a case of a couple's treatment, and defines the important clinical elements encountered in analytic work with disturbed and disorganized couples. The concepts of pathological organization, psychic retreat, the death instinct, and projective identification are discussed in reference to the treatment of couples. Modern Kleinian Therapy is a theoretical and clinical approach which utilizes the main elements of Kleinian technique for patients in reduced frequency treatment, often with more severe psychological disturbance, and in the context of either individual or couples settings. Severely neurotic, borderline, narcissistic, and even psychotic couples are common in our private practice settings. As a result, we are used to being the referee, peacekeeper, policeman, savior, negotiator, translator, decoy, diplomat, provocateur, container, and healer, depending on what type of transference profile is bestowed upon the analyst by either each individual and/or by the couple.

However, these transference modes can be difficult to handle owing to the rigid projective identification mechanisms found in the pathological organization couples so often use to maintain their unique level of psychic equilibrium. Using case material, the author shows how to work with hard-to-reach couples by means of an analytic exploration of the couple's pathological organization, the associated dynamics of the death instinct, and the last-resort defense of the psychic retreat.

In Chapter 8, couples therapy is again explored from a Kleinian perspective, with one extensive case used for illustration. The concepts of pathological organization and psychic retreat are shown to be valuable in conducting psychoanalytic couples treatment. Issues of transference and counter-transference are addressed as well as the endless cycles of projective identification that ground most couples in their mutual system of unconscious functioning. These patterns of relational repetition in which specific roles, wishes, and conflicts are played out can be a source of life-sustaining nourishment and growth-directed interaction or a foundation of destructive, rigid, and stagnant non-relating. Analytic couples treatment can help the latter return to the former or to shift the latter to the former for the first time. This is only possible if the deeper unconscious struggles that make up the pathological organization are addressed.

In Chapter 9, the author considers the manifestations and struggles of those individuals who are not able or willing to shift to depressive position functioning.

This developmental drama is examined by looking at the creative dynamics of a recent film. The 2010 film *Another Year* provides a valuable opportunity to consider the terrifying anxiety and despair some individuals face when making the transition from the paranoid-schizoid position (Klein 1946) to the depressive position (Klein 1935, 1940). Many are unable, many are unwilling, but some do take a step into more whole object functioning with success. However, some feel they have stepped into a new, unknown abyss of intense grief and separation from which they quickly retreat back to the familiar catastrophic pain of the paranoid-schizoid experience. Issues of pathological projective identification and the elements of grief and loss regarding the object as container are addressed. In addition, the two-stage process of depressive position development and the two stages of containment are discussed.

In Chapter 10, the author uses a recent film to showcase how psychoanalytic understanding may be used to clarify the otherwise confusing and overwhelming actions of some more disturbed individuals. The film *Good Neighbors* is explored from a Kleinian psychoanalytic perspective. The characters are understood as suffering from a variety of narcissistic problems that leave them constantly exposed to a sense of abandonment, loss, and internal fragmentation. They must use others to reorganize themselves and piece back together their scattered and broken emotional experience of self. A destructive reaction to severe loss and a lack of self-identity drives a predatory mindset in which others are used as fuel for a psychological fire that is always threatening to extinguish, leaving them cold and alone.

Chapter 11 examines the difficulties of treating patients who consciously desire help in living a more organized, integrated, and fulfilling life but unconsciously fight the analyst's efforts at shifting their pathological object-relational dynamics. These patients resort to intense splitting and projective identification defense systems based around the death instinct and pathological organizations to retain their internal status quo. The resulting transference maneuvers can pull the analyst into two primary counter-transference states. Responding to the patient's primitive paranoid or depressive splitting and projective processes, the analyst will slip into the grip of exaggerated versions of the life-or-death instinct and be tempted to act out in one or the other direction. Case material is used for illustration.

Chapter 12 looks at how the pathological rewards of the paranoid-schizoid position (Klein 1946) are too gratifying for some patients to discard. In addition, the depressive (Klein 1935, 1940) challenges of dealing with loss, the reality of unavailable, broken, or abusive objects, and the threat of conflict that comes with self-confidence are all too much to take on. Thus, these more resistive and hard-to-reach patients elect to stay loyal to existing states of pre-depressive object-relational conflict and current patterns of psychic equilibrium.

This type of patient presents a particularly difficult transference profile that evokes specific counter-transference states. The analyst is invariably drawn into siding with either exaggerated aspects of the life instinct or exaggerated aspects of the death instinct. Unless one is very careful, it is easy to enact one or both of these projective identification-based scenarios with the patient. Ultimately, the analyst must side with neither and allow the patient to play out their end goal while still providing a balance of analytic interest and interpretation. Sometimes, this will facilitate a working-through process and sometimes it will not. Case material is used for illustration.

Part I

Clinical aspects of loss and disconnection

Low-frequency Modern Kleinian Therapy and one patient's somatic retreat from unbearable loss

This chapter will focus on the application of the regular Kleinian technique to difficult and disturbed patients who are only able or willing to attend once or twice a week (Waska 2006, 2011b). I will demonstrate with clinical material how there is no real need to modify the technique. However, in low frequency cases, certain aspects of pathology, of transference, and of defense become highlighted and heightened, so certain aspects of technique must also be highlighted.

The Modern Kleinian Therapy approach is a clinical model of here-and-now, moment-to-moment focus on transference, counter-transference, and unconscious phantasy to assist difficult patients in low frequency therapy to notice, accept, understand, and resolve their unconscious self- and object-conflict states. Projective identification is often the cornerstone of the more complex transference state (Waska 2004) and therefore is the central target of therapeutic intervention and interpretation.

A great deal of patients being seen in today's private practice settings are mired in the primitive zone of paranoid and narcissistic functioning without access to the internal vision of a pleasurable object with which to merge without catastrophe. These are patients who are using vigorous levels of defense against the more erotic, pleasurable, and connective elements of relationship just as they are massively defending against the fears of conflict, aggression, and growth. In addition, this is a state of psychic conflict so intense that it may in some cases create psychic deficit.

Clinically, we see many patients who tend to quickly subsume us and whatever we do or say into their pathological organization (Spillius 1988) with its familiar cast of internal characters. Modern Kleinian Therapy focuses on the interpretation of this particular transference process by investigating the unconscious phantasy conflicts at play and highlighting the more direct moment-to-moment transference usually mobilized by projective identification dynamics. Bion's (1962a) ideas regarding the interpersonal aspects of projective identification, the idea of projective identification as the foundation of most transference states (Waska 2010a, 2010b, 2010c), and the concept of projective identification as the first line of defense against psychic loss (Waska 2002, 2010d) difference, or separation all form the theoretical base of my clinical approach. Taking theory into the clinical realm, I find interpreting the how and the why of the patient's phantasy conflicts in the here-and-now combined with linkage to original infantile experiences to be the best approach with such patients under these more limiting clinical situations.

In doing so, the main thrust of the analyst's observations and interpretations remains focused on the patient's efforts to disrupt the establishment of analytic contact (Waska 2007). We strive to move the patient into a new experience of clarity, vulnerability, reflection, independence, change, and choice. Analytic contact is defined as sustained periods of mutual existence between self and object not excessively colored by destructive aggression or destructive defense. These are moments between patient and analyst when the elements of love, hate, and knowledge as well as the life-and-death instincts are in "good-enough" balance as to not fuel, enhance, or validate the patient's internal conflicts and phantasies in those very realms. These are new moments of contact between self and other, either in the mind of the patient or in the actual interpersonal realm between patient and analyst. Internal dynamics surrounding giving, taking, and learning as well as the parallel phantasies of being given to, having to relinquish, and being known are all elements that are usually severely out of psychic balance with these more challenging patients. Analytic contact is the moment in which analyst and patient achieve some degree of peace, stability, or integration in these areas.

So, analytic contact is the term for our constant quest or invitation to each patient for the found, allowed, and cultivated experiences that are new or less contaminated by the fossils of past internal drama, danger, and desire. These moments, in turn, provide for a chance of more lasting change, life, and difference or at least a consideration that these elements are possible and not poison. Paranoid (Klein 1946) and depressive (Klein 1935, 1940) anxieties tend to be stirred up as the patient's safe and controlled psychic equilibrium (Spillius and Feldman 1989) comes into question. Acting out, abrupt termination, intense resistance, and excessive reliance on projective identification are common and create easy blind spots and patterns of enactment for the analyst.

While Modern Kleinian Therapy is fundamentally no different than the practice of Kleinian psychoanalysis, due to the limitations of reduced frequency, more severe pathology, and external blocks such as health insurance limitations and personal financial limitations, a greater flexibility is required in the overall treatment setting. In addition, there is a greater need to notice the ongoing and immediate impact of unconscious phantasy, internal conflict, and transference that occurs in the analytic relationship. Careful monitoring of countertransference for the presence of projective identification-based communication is an important Modern Kleinian Therapy technique. The importance of combining interpretations of current here-and-now transference and phantasy with occasional genetic links as a therapeutic hybrid approach is also a modification of sorts unique to Modern Kleinian Therapy. However, this is more a question of emphasis than a new or radical theoretical shift or unique technique.

Case material

Norm is a thirty-five-year-old man who came to me for help with feelings of depression and anxiety. I had seen him for seven sessions at this point, once a week without the analytic couch. Norm told me his doctors suggested he seek help for the psychological aspects of his recent symptoms. He reported a wide array of troubling pains and soreness, including back pain, leg weakness, dizziness, shoulder troubles, arm tingling, shortness of breath, chest pains, exhaustion, trouble sleeping, and balance problems. While he had a history of physical problems dating back many years, a great deal of these symptoms had started or intensified over the past year.

Norm's parents divorced when he was six. Afterwards, his uncle became his father figure. Norm felt very close to him while growing up and still does. He does not say much about the effects of this history, so I am the one left to wonder about it and give it value and pain. Norm's mother developed breast cancer when he was ten years old. She went in and out of remission until she died when Norm was thirty years old. Last year, Norm's uncle was diagnosed with a terminal brain tumor and was given a year to live. Norm does not say much about his feelings in general and when he relayed these sad events with these important figures in his life he didn't show much emotion. I commented on this and he said, "I think I just got used to it with my mother since it went on for so long." What Norm does show emotion about is his physical status and the problems he thinks he may have. He says he "is really worried about what might be wrong and if it is serious. The doctors say they have done all the tests and found nothing wrong but I still have all these strange feelings and the weakness and pain. I think I should get more tests."

I suggested that he might be having a somatic reaction to the ongoing grief and loss in his life. Norm said he thought it could be but he "still worries about what might be going on." He told me that the referring physician told him he was stressed and having anxiety reactions. Norm said he wasn't sure if that was right but was willing to try therapy "if it would stop all these terrible feelings in my body."

Norm was very athletic as a teen and played on numerous teams. He won several awards competitively and "loved to play ball." I asked him if his mother's ongoing illness made it hard to concentrate on sports or school when he was growing up. He said he didn't think about it too much except when she had to go back into the hospital for treatments. I asked if his father, uncle, mother, or anyone else talked to him about this difficult situation. Norm said no one ever did. I asked if he had ever tried to bring up his feelings or questions with his mother. Norm told me he "never did because I didn't want to be a burden. I thought she had enough to think about and deal with without me adding to her troubles."

I interpreted that he felt his needs and worries were selfish and were burdens on others so he kept them to himself, but that way of coping and protecting others left him alone and overwhelmed with his anxiety and grief. He said,

I can see what you mean but I just did my thing in sports and school. The only time I really felt concerned was when she had a relapse and had to go to the hospital. Most of the time, she seemed healthy and didn't talk about the cancer so I felt okay. The only time I really felt badly about it was years later when she was told she only had six months to live. Then, it was final and real. I really felt sad then. It was awful. She had cancer for so long and I had grown up with her that way that I didn't really think of her as sick until the end.

Norm's mother died when he was thirty. When Norm was twenty, his grandfather died after a battle with cancer. Norm was quite close to him. Norm was playing basketball a few weeks after finding out that his grandfather had cancer and he felt some leg pain. Norm played again the next day and felt some back pain. The third day he played another basketball game, got changed, and suddenly experienced an excoriating pain in his back and leg. He ended up at the hospital that night. For the next month he was on painkillers and in and out of the hospital, unable to walk. Overall, the doctors found some problems with his back but nothing serious. However, due to his symptoms he was told that they could perform exploratory surgery but because of how young he was they recommended no surgery. He was told to avoid straining his back until it hopefully recovered on its own. So, Norm stopped playing sports and confined his activities to going to work and minor shopping or short walks.

In listening to Norm describe this scenario, I noted that he did not convey any sense of frustration, anger, or anxiety about having to curtail much of his active life at such a young age. He was without emotion and seemed to just adjust to it. I said it seemed like what he must have done with his mother, just trying to adjust and somehow have no feelings about something shocking and unwanted. Norm said he "knew there was nothing I could do about it and I didn't want to make it worse so I had to go along with it."

In the counter-transference, I noticed I was becoming the voice of life and the one who had feelings, wanting more than life was offering. I made this interpretation of the projective identification-based transference and Norm said he knew what I meant but had felt helpless to expect more, given what had happened to his back. I said I was surprised he gave up so easily, given how important sports and activities were to him while growing up.

I said,

You seemed to have had this emotional reaction to your grandfather but you were showing the pain and the utter helplessness you felt through your body instead of being able to talk about it and feel it. A strong driving force in your life was gone and your spirit was broken. But, you tried to be neutral and accepting about it. Yet, the pain persisted in your body.

Norm listened in an interested way but didn't say much to elaborate. I asked him if he ever considered the back incident to be related to his grandfather's illness.

Norm said he had not but, now that I had brought it up and drew the parallel to his mother and uncle, he could see how it might be a factor.

What he was referring to was a line of similar tragedy and resulting physical reactions throughout his life. When his mother was dying, he went to the emergency room with severe swallowing problems and stomach aches. He went to many specialists and was told he had irritable bowel syndrome and acid reflux. On the one hand he felt relieved at finally "knowing what the problem is" but he still doesn't quite believe the doctors were right and "perhaps they didn't find something else that was really the cause." Yet he seemed to really respond to the concrete knowledge of an actual physical diagnosis. I said, "Maybe that is easier than so many intense feelings for your dying mother and her loss that you can't totally understand or pin down. You feel more in control with a physical label." Norm said, "Yes. I like it when I know what it is and can move on." I said, "You haven't been able to move on from your mother's death and your grandfather's death. We can try and solve that."

After his mother died of cancer some six years ago, Norm told me he was sad but not surprised, and glad his mother was no longer in pain. He said he felt as if a very long story was now over, the story of his mother's twenty-year battle with cancer. I added that he had been in that war every day for twenty years and it had taken its toll on him, but all the feelings seemed to have become stored or hidden in his body and in his fear of illness. He spent the years focusing on his body and what might be wrong with it. At this point, when I said this, it came to me that he was also identifying with his mother as well as reliving his conflicted childhood focus. Just like his mother, he was always worried, wondering about his health and what was wrong, and scared that the doctors had missed something. And, as a child, on some level, he was always focused on his mother's body and now, as an adult, he was always focused on his body.

Shortly after his mother died, Norm developed a great variety of physical symptoms, mostly related to his back. He felt great pain in his lower back and weakness and pain in his legs. He also felt shortness of breath and dizziness, as well as other symptoms of panic attacks. As the back pain increased, he started to visit specialists. Eventually, he ended up having back surgery. During the preliminary tests, the doctors discovered a bulging disc. They told him they had never seen one so damaged and wondered if he had suffered a traumatic accident or had tried to lift some incredible weight again and again. He had done neither. In fact, he lived a fairly sedentary life.

After the first surgery he was still in some pain, so after about a year he had a second back operation. Now, Norm feels better but is very careful to not exert any pressure or strain on his back. Thus he takes virtually no exercise, no sports, and makes sure to not lift anything. He feels he cannot ever interview for any job that would require him to sit for a length of time. I listened to him and noticed the degree of conviction with which he had given up so much in life and settled for a limited lifestyle. I was almost convinced of how this was necessary by the way he told me the story, the transference method he was relating (Steiner 2000).

But then I asked him if his doctors, surgeons, and specialists had all told him to never exercise and if they had told him his condition was still that dire, restricted, and fragile. Norm said no, but that he "just could feel that in my body and I don't want to push myself to a point of doing something damaging." I interpreted that he had given up on himself as an active person and labeled himself as dangerously closed to collapse, even though none of his specialists or surgeons had told him so.

Again, I was speaking for life, activity, and hope while Norm seemed to cling to decline, danger, and doom. This was an example of internal conflicts regarding the life-and-death instincts emerging clinically and the role which need, desire, dependence, and hope seemed to play in his life in this destructive manner.

About six months ago, Norm's uncle was unexpectedly diagnosed with a terminal brain tumor. Immediately afterwards, Norm started to feel dizzy and weak. He has been convinced that there is something "fundamentally unsound" with him physically. In listening to him, it sounded as if he started to have a series of anxiety attacks, followed by a conviction that he "has something drastically wrong physically." I thought that he was in a way taking over his mother's identity, experiencing the same feelings and fears she must have had over the years (Grinberg 1990). I made this interpretation and said that perhaps this was a desperate attempt to stay connected to her. He told me he understood what I meant and "it makes sense" but that "I still have a conviction that there is something wrong with my body and a breakdown of either my back or something else because of all the pain, numbness, tingling, and soreness I feel in all these different areas of my body."

In the counter-transference, I sometimes feel like yelling at Norm and trying to force or convince him that all these somatic issues are really his hidden grief, anger, sorrow, and anxiety over not having these vital people in his life any more (Joseph 1987; Grinberg 1962, 1968). I want to shout, "It's about cancer, loss, and fear, not mysterious back pain and dizziness!" In noting these feelings and not acting out on them, over time I have come to think of this counter-transference as representing how Norm wanted to yell out as a teen to someone for help, since no one was ever talking about the terrible situation with his grandfather, his mother, and now with his uncle as well.

In other words, I think that, through projective identification (Steiner 2008), Norm was putting his unexpressed anxiety and anger into me because he felt scared and guilty to own these conflicts. I think he both wants to jettison these dangerous feelings into me so as to never have to deal with them but is also making an unconscious communication and a hopeful move to have me express them. Eventually, he may join me in the process and re-own them as his own. In the transference, he is also now the one ignoring the obvious, denying the painful reality of loss and trauma just as he felt everyone else was ignoring it when he was young. Finally, he is able to merge or stay with his mother by experiencing the same types of symptoms and worries that he may have imagined his mother to have, such as "this could be serious," "this might be something fatal," "I hope the doctors haven't missed something," "maybe I should get more tests," and "I know they told me I am okay right now but I still feel like there could be something terribly wrong."

Norm has also told me about his envy of other seemingly "normal families who don't seem to have had to go through all these terrible health problems. Everyone was healthy when the kids grew up and everyone is still alive now. Sometimes, I find myself wondering why!" When I tell him he is talking about a great deal of anguish, anger, resentment, and sorrow, Norm is quick to backtrack and tell me he didn't have it that bad and that lots of other families have troubles too. He adds that it is wrong to feel jealous or angry because this is simply his life experience and he shouldn't feel cheated. I interpret that he feels guilty about showing me the extent of his strong feelings and now wants to take them back and smooth things over. I add that he may have had those feelings for a long time and felt so guilty about burdening his mother that he tried to keep them to himself then too. When he still tells me he is "managing okay and doing all right" I interpret that he resists my compassion and understanding because it may lead to him feeling overwhelmed by all these feelings and also thinking he is being a burden on me and overwhelming me. In response Norm told me,

> I always felt so bad for my mother. She was a single mom without much money, raising all of us and suffering with cancer every day. I thought I would be selfish if I ever complained about anything or asked her how she felt. She never said anything about her feelings so I thought I better not ask or I would be making her feel bad. I feel like she worked so hard and was such a good mother and then lost out on enjoying the rest of her life. It seems so unfair!

At that point, Norm broke down and cried. This was quite a different moment in the transference in that he was allowing himself to feel the loss and sorrow and sharing it with me. He shifted away from his pathological organization and somatic retreat and, for a moment, related to me openly about the terrible separation, and he was challenging his conviction that speaking was hurtful.

My sense of Norm's unconscious coping method, the structure of his psychic retreat (Steiner 1993), was that he wanted to know the answers to this somatic "thing" that was happening to him. This quest seemed to protect him from facing the knowledge of the person who had left him and the person who was dying, a psychological loss of unbearable magnitude (Steiner 1990).

Most sessions were taken up with Norm starting off talking about his physical symptoms. If he was silent and I asked him how he was feeling, Norm would tell me the degree of pain he felt in his legs, the soreness in his back, or the level of dizziness he had that day. I felt compelled to force him to face reality, that he had lost these important figures in his life and was in the middle of yet another loss that no doubt was triggering his original grief experience with his mother. I wanted to show him how angry, grief stricken, and upset he was. When I did so by saying he was probably having a hard time hearing about his uncle's latest round of chemotherapy, he would agree for a moment, but then tell me, "we just don't talk about it. I don't want to bring it up and make my uncle feel bad."

I interpreted that Norm probably felt that way with his mother and grandfather too. Norm told me he had indeed felt that way and he tried his best to not "burden them." I interpreted that he was in fact emotionally burdened and overwhelmed by these events and needed someone to be there for him, which is part of why he came to see me. But then he ends up trying to be nice and not take up emotional space with me or his uncle. I said his feelings and focus end up on his body where he feels something is wrong or falling apart instead of having to focus on how his heart is breaking and his emotional life is falling apart. Norm told me he understood what I meant but he "cannot stop thinking about what might be wrong" with him and "if the doctors missed something."

Norm hasn't had a job for some time and feels that no one would hire him with his history of back problems. He sees himself as without value and essentially damaged beyond repair. I interpreted this as his way of seeing himself as defeated and without life, a way he could stay close with his dead and dying family. If he felt more alive he would have to end up feeling as if he was moving ahead and saying goodbye to them. Here, I was interpreting his conflicts with both his actual external family and his internal family.

Rubin (2004) notes that contemporary Kleinians, in comparison with more traditional Kleinians, place a much greater emphasis on real versus phantasy conflicts with others as well as according greater value to the effects of early family pathology. I think that this is true of a general trend in the Kleinian approach but also a continued misunderstanding of how Klein and her followers actually worked. Klein herself wrote of the actual effects of the infant's external family experiences and how the infant might take in that experience and then project the combination of real-life interaction with internal reaction back on to the object, creating a new and distorted object to once again react to. Klein and her followers spoke of how the healthy mother–child bond could mitigate this from becoming too dark or overwhelming and instead help install an internal sense of hope, confidence, and trust. This would be the foundation of normal projective identification and the creation of positive unconscious phantasies about self and other.

Unconscious phantasies are internal, unconscious object relationships between self and other that underlie all mental processes. These phantasies are the expression of conflicts and defenses surrounding love, hate, and knowledge, and shape the balance of the life-and-death instincts. These elements of human struggle and desire are what psychoanalytic treatment hopes to bring into more conscious awareness followed by increased integration. In working with Norm, I noticed my analytic efforts to do so became colored by my counter-transference urge to force him to know and face the painful truth about his objects. I believe he was trying to preserve his internal objects by making them part of his somatic state.

Internal objects are unconscious images and version of external people and situations that the subject has intense emotional reactions to, both positive and negative. Throughout life, the subject projects their various feelings and thoughts about self and other on to their valued or despised object, and then internalizes the combination of reality and their distortion back inside. This starts another cycle of unconscious coping and reaction to that new internal object which is then projected again. Thus, there is a never-ending recycling of one's vision of self and other that one is continuously organizing, relating, and reacting to, both externally and internally, both intra-psychically and interpersonally. In the paranoid-schizoid position, these internal objects are often fragmented part objects rather than the more integrated whole objects experienced in the depressive position.

Norm developed fragmented non-symbolic states of mind that existed in his body instead of his mind. This allowed him to avoid the terrible sense of unbearable loss he would face in a more symbolic depressive position experience of his life. The paranoid-schizoid mode is usually found in more borderline, narcissistic, or psychotic patients but we all exist within this mode to some degree or can easily regress to it under trying circumstances. Klein believed the healthy transition from the paranoid-schizoid experience (Klein 1946) to more whole-object depressive functioning (Klein 1935, 1940) had much to do with the constitutional balance of the life-and-death instincts and the external conditions of optimal mothering. The primary anxiety in this position has to do with survival of the self rather than concern for the object.

For Norm, he seems to retreat to this fear of self-survival to avoid the overwhelming loss and anxiety of the depressive position, where he would need to experience, accept, and grieve the terrible loss of his internal and external family of loved ones.

Based on the transference and my resulting counter-transference, my clinical impression is that Norm is over-reliant on projective identification as a method of surviving these conflicts and fears (Steiner 1989, 2011). However, the type of projective identification he depends on leaves him in constant fear and without internal stability or security. Rigid, excessive, or perverse forms of projective identification offer brief, illusionary moments of safety from persecutory or guilty phantasies but also create the very terror that one is trying to evade.

Formulated by Klein and first discussed in her 1946 paper, projective identification is an unconscious phantasy in which aspects of the self or internal object are attributed to another internal or external object. These phantasies can be positive or negative in nature and may or may not have interpersonal aspects to them that engage others in patterns of relating that confirm the core phantasy elements. Besides attributing aspects of the self to another, projective identification may also involve finding and owning aspects of the other. Thus, the motives of projective identification are many and may be part of healthy normal development and relating, or be part of destructive, defensive pathology. In reflecting upon Norm's transference state, it seemed as if he would shift rather rapidly between different roles and motives in the projective process, leaving me to either experience multiple unwanted aspects of himself or to react to multiple versions of his internal objects. In other words, at times in the projective identification-based transference, Norm took on the role of his mother not wanting to talk about anything emotional, a re-creation of his mother struggling with physical worries and assorted ailments but trying to act as if everything was okay. Other moments involved Norm relating like a child who wanted someone to speak for him, a child who didn't want to face the terrible reality of his life. Still, at other moments, he seemed to convey the conviction that any independent move, personal statement, or sign of growth would endanger others. Thus, it was better to stay quiet, passive, and without any significant opinion or difference.

In the counter-transference, I found myself on the other end of these various states, feeling initially like acting them out, feeling confused and dragged into it, but then slowly making sense of it (Racker 1957). With Klein's discovery of projective identification, the transference is seen by Kleinians as an unconscious method of communicating to, retreating from, loving, or attacking the analyst. In addition, modern Kleinian theory includes the interpersonal pressures put upon the analyst during the more intense moments of transference. Thus, the analyst will constantly be affected in the counter-transference. Therefore, enactments of various degrees are unavoidable. In this regard, the counter-transference is now seen as a valuable and crucial tool with which to better understand the exact nature of the patient's conflict and from which to better construct accurate interpretations. With Norm, I often felt as if I was fighting for the life instincts, the chance to grieve, and the realization of love that was lost, but I also noticed the almost aggressive manner in which I wanted him to realize it and accept it. This alerted me to the possible feelings of anger, envy, resentment, and desire that were all very much unwanted and pushed over into me.

Riesenberg-Malcolm (1990) has noted that if the mother's alpha function breaks down or is censored or shut off as in Norm's case, the infant, child, or teen is left without a healthy projective identification system to process anxiety. As a result, there is a sense of inner fragmentation and idealized false objects are created upon which to depend. Roth (1994) believes these patients do so to avoid knowledge of the actual nature of their object. For Norm, I think he felt alone without his mother's ability to process her own anxiety and share her ability to contain it. Thus, Norm was left without adequate containment and dreaded the knowledge of his mother's true condition, an emotionally frail and physically compromised woman without a husband upon whom to depend. Thus, to cope, Norm projected idealized false maternal objects into his body but they lacked any real qualities. He stripped them of any symbolic function in order to shield himself from the pain of a broken or dying mother and to shield his mother from his needs and aggression. Yet this resulted in Norm feeling possessed by strange, dreadful, unknown entities in his body that he could not contain or control. Norm was left in a state of nameless dread (Bion 1962b) and this brought on organismic panic (Pao 1977) that left him overwhelmed, persecuted, and lost.

The maternal container must be open and receptive or the sender feels shut out and alone with unbearable internal anxiety. The basic function of the interpreting analyst is a model of receiving, containing, modifying, translating, and returning that provides the patient with this fundamental infant/mother experience. There are many ways in which this container/contained cycle can fail, be perverted, or put to the test during the patient's early family experiences as well as duplicated in the transference situation (Joseph 1985; Steiner 1996). This was part of the pushy counter-transference I felt and the desperate rush Norm felt and conveyed to me about what to do and how to get rid of his anxiety.

Without any real containment, Norm floated in this limbo of panic and uncertainty. However, over time, this has become a pathological organization. Pathological organizations are rigid and intense systems of defense used to avoid unbearable persecutory and depressive anxieties and result in a distancing from others and from internal and external reality. Some more difficult-to-reach patients are involved in highly destructive narcissistic actions of certain parts of the self against other parts of the self, resulting in a variety of sadomasochistic, perverse, or addictive character profiles. Other patients exhibit a desperate attempt to create a fragile and precarious retreat from both paranoid and depressive fears but eliminate any hopeful object-relational balance that comes from the normal experiences of both positions. Pathological organizations are destructive states of psychic equilibrium, providing a temporary sense of control and respite but ultimately removing the patient from the healing aspects of reality and the working through of both paranoid and depressive issues. The idea of psychic retreats is a parallel concept that explains how patients seek a protective shell, haven, or refuge from overwhelming phantasies of loss, annihilation, persecution, and guilt. In treatment, these patients are stuck and out of reach. The patient feels safely out of touch with reality and from their threatening or threatened objects, but also out of touch with the understanding and help of the analyst.

Norm's pathological organization centered around his body and his conviction of something being wrong that was not yet understood. This internal system of psychic equilibrium (Joseph 1989) in which he never felt as if he knew what was going on with his body defended him from knowing what had happened to his mother and now his uncle, and knowing how he felt about it. He would rather live with nameless dread than face a named dread, the known loss of the depressive position and the psychological trauma of his dying family.

Knowledge, knowing, and learning are a central component to the Kleinian theory of what makes up the human psyche. Klein placed the desire to know the object alongside the life-and-death instincts as fundamental in understanding human motivation. The subject is curious, envious, and wanting to understand the workings of the object. This creates a desire to be inside the other to taste, test, share, own, and be the other. In healthy development, this involves a thirst for knowledge, a drive to find out, and a talent to solve problems through learning. The unknown becomes something that fuels growth and exploration. In unhealthy or pathological states, the unknown is unbearable, envy of the other takes over, and a desperate and aggressive attack is launched to find entry into the object and take what is inside. This may result in claustrophobic phantasies, fears of reprisal, revenge, and retribution, as well as a sense of self as inferior and without, that others know and one is clueless and left out. Anxieties about knowing may cause learning disorders and fuel an aggressive quest to know. This may lead to obsessive disorders that require knowing at all times with a resulting feeling of terrible guilt. In addition, experiences of annihilation, fragmentation, and of being unfixed and uncontained may occur. In treatment, many patients display the resistance or fear of knowing themselves, feel trespassed by our wanting to know about them, and rely on a primitive system of withholding or of projecting what is inside-out to protect themselves from others knowing more about them.

Grinberg (1977) has described how many borderline patients have experienced, either in phantasy and/or with actual external caregivers, traumatic separation, and loss. This has usually been based in the infantile experience of a mother who has not been able or willing to receive, contain, or modify the infant's unorganized inner conflicts. This idea of Grinberg's is based on Bion's container concept (Bion 1962a, 1962bb) which has been elaborated upon by other Kleinians. The concept has been defined as a fundamental psychic state of mind in which the infant feels helpless in the face of loss, abandonment, or rejection by the object, leaving the infant in a blank emotional void and an internal sense of meaninglessness.

Grinberg (1968) notes how primitive patients are prone to acting out in search of and in reaction to the felt lack of a containing object that can sustain their separation anxiety, grief, guilt, and loss. I would add that this acting out is not just part of a search for the lost object but an angry retribution and revenge as well for the perceived abandonment and betrayal. Thus, the containing object, the ideal good object, even if found, is never enough and always at fault. This creates a persecutory cycle of paranoid phantasies and unbearable guilt in which the lost object is now purposely neglectful and absent, and the patient is always hungry and always has blood on their hands. This brings back the most fundamental and terrible infantile state of mind of when absence was intolerable and the missing object was no longer a good object temporarily absent, but a persecutory non-object cruelly missing and permanently gone, yet forever haunting the empty, hungry, and desperate child's mind and heart.

Steiner (1992) and other Kleinians have noted the early, more immature stage of the depressive position in which the patient has great difficulty tolerating and accepting the loss of the needed object. Denial, manic, defenses, or narcissistic and pathological organizations that defend against paranoid collapse are all common. This is similar to Quinodoz's (1996) concept of untamed solitude as well as Palacio Espasa's (2002) idea of the more para-psychotic and para-depressive phantasies of catastrophic, irreparable, and life-deadening or life-draining states of loss. Only when the patient is able and willing to face, tolerate, and integrate the actual and/or imagined betrayal, traumatic loss, and perceived rejection can they move towards the more mature stage of the depressive position where forgiveness, hope, and a livable future exist.

In erecting his somatic containment, a pathological organization in which Norm attempted to establish a grief-free zone where he merely needed to know what was wrong with his body in order to quickly shut off his physical experiences of anxiety, he found himself lost without the true translating function of the mother container. I offered him the chance to talk about what was really going on, something he wanted as a child but also dreaded and avoided so as to not burden his mother and not have to feel the sorrow himself. This is now being repeated with his uncle and with myself; but, when faced with having the opportunity to finally face these feelings and experiences, he turned away to avoid the depressive pain that would emerge with it.

Norm retreated to the non-symbolic pseudo containment of his somatic phantasy and then expected me to quickly help him identify exactly what was wrong. I interpreted that I wanted him to know what was emotionally wrong and he wanted me to tell him what was physically wrong and find out what to do about it. He said that "even if it is psychological, I want to know what to do to make it go away as soon as possible." I said, "You can't make the loss of your mother and uncle go away. But we can face it together and work on how to live with it." He said, "I don't want to. I just want to stop having all these problems with my body." Thus, I noticed that we both became impatient with each other about what we wanted and what we thought was the best goal. I seemed to stand for the life instinct and the quest for emotional knowledge, and Norm seemed to stand for the death instinct, trying to always deny, destroy, or denude the emotional connection with his lost objects and annihilate any need, dependency, or feeling for them. He wanted to exchange that known lost love in his heart for an unknown dire enemy located in his body.

Regarding the life-and-death instincts, Modern Kleinian Therapy (Waska 2010a, 2011a, 2011b) clinically considers the distinct anti-life, anti-growth, or anti-change force that seems to have the upper hand in some patients. The death instinct seems to arise most violently in situations of envy, difference, separation, or challenge to enduring pathological organizations and pathological forms of psychic equilibrium.

Hanna Segal (1993) has defined it as the individual's reactions to needs. Either one can seek satisfaction for the needs and accept and deal with the frustrations and problems that come with those efforts. This is life-affirming action or the actions of the life instinct. It is life promoting and object seeking. Eventually, this leads from concerns about the survival of the self to concerns about the well-being of the other.

The other reaction to needs is the drive to annihilate the self that has needs, and to annihilate others and things that represent those needs. Kleinians see envy as a prime aspect of the death instinct and that early external experiences of deprivation and trauma play as big a role as internal, constitutional factors in the ultimate balance between the life-and-death forces.

For Norm, he seems trapped in between and reluctant to emerge as it appears too overwhelming and devastating (Steiner 2008). Yet, the few sessions we have had together show that he is cautiously willing to slowly consider facing that frightening new way of remembering his objects, mourning them, and finding a new way to bond with them.

Chapter 2

Working with psychotic process

Noticing the counter-transference and transference dynamic in early analytic treatment

The initial phase of psychoanalytic treatment can be quite difficult for both patient and analyst. For the patient, there is the conviction that the analyst will simply be another in the long line of repeat characters in their transference vision of the world, a place where the roles never change and the play never stops. This conviction forms the core conflict, the basic resistance to change, and the projective identification pattern.

For the analyst, there is the immediate confusion and anxiety of being partner to this transference confusion and web of rigid psychic demands that have not yet been discovered. The analyst is simply the new surprise guest in the patient's internal world and has to feel his way through that unfamiliar darkness. Counter-transference is essential in this respect and careful monitoring of the patient's responses to interpretation is important.

In this chapter, I will share the clinical elements I encountered as I tried to understand the results of establishing, or at least trying to establish, a relationship with one new patient. I have now seen Paul for fifteen sessions, so the nature of the analytic contact (Waska 2007, 2010a, 2010b) is frail and somewhat undefined. However, a transference profile has emerged and much progress has occurred regarding anxiety and phantasy conflict. How Paul wants both closeness, change, power, learning, and the freedom to think and feel without dread or guilt is something I am just starting to understand. At the same time, he is preventing, numbing, or destroying those psychic possibilities in a deliberate unconscious manner. Thus, from the lens of counter-transference, I am noticing many ways Paul is making efforts to engage or disengage with me.

Paul is twenty-two years old. When he came to see me, he was very nervous that he was going to kill himself. He told me he would suddenly think, "You will jump off the bridge later this week." Paul had a bottle of anti-anxiety medication and he heard himself think, "You will take an overdose." He was scared and confused about this and wanted my help. Paul told me he also felt he "knew what most people were thinking" and "knew people are always thinking about me, scrutinizing my choices."

Paul thinks he is an undiscovered genius, that he is superior and smarter than all others, and that he has an ability to "influence all those around him." He has felt much worse over the past year since his breakup with his girlfriend and being told he was not accepted on the college basketball team. But, in response to my asking about his feelings, he quickly devalued, minimized, and neutralized the importance of these situations.

Initially, Paul told me he felt loved by his family, with whom he still lives. He used to take frequent doses of psychedelic mushrooms and smoked pot every day. Paul is scared of going off to college later in the year, moving away from his parents, and away from treatment. He thinks he will be overwhelmed by the social aspects, "not able to find a place to hide and be by myself." He thinks he will be unable to date because he "never is willing to be involved in small talk." Paul has many delusions about being "super-smart and able to know things that others don't," feeling superior to others, and convinced that he is "the chosen one." When he plays the piano, he is sure he is composing the best song ever played, that he will be discovered and become world famous overnight. At the same time, Paul feels others are always judging him, looking down on him, and able to tell what he is thinking. He feels he never fits in.

My impression of the initial transference situation was characteristic of early phase analytic treatment. There is much to gather, understand, and tolerate. Out of that confusion there are provisional interpretations to make regarding the transference as well as towards the patient's apparent core unconscious conflicts and their base phantasy state. These initial interpretations grow out, in part, of the counter-transference which is influenced by the ways the patient uses us, relates to us, and locates us within their primary object-relational phantasy.

With Paul, he was quick to have me fix him, label him, and eliminate the bad feelings he felt inside. He wanted me to help him in his desperate quest to stop feeling as if everyone turned away from him or thought badly of him. On the one hand, Paul was quite bright and eager to learn about the possible source of his problems. Thus, he asked me my opinions about him, researched the internet for answers, and came up with interesting theories. This all made him look like a motivated patient working hard at change. But, in the transference, it was all done in a mechanical fashion. He kept his distance with intellectual conjecture, anxiously repeated tales of constant judgment from self and others, and demands for psychiatric diagnosis that might confirm what he read on the internet.

Paul told me he

> really fit the description of a schizophrenic, especially the part about feeling like I am the chosen one. I have always felt better than others. Other people tend to be stupid and never see the finer points of life that I notice. I have always known there is probably a higher level that we are not aware of, like in the movie *The Matrix*. But most people don't realize that. I don't like talking to anyone because they just want to talk about the weather or other useless information. I think there are very important things going on that are worth thinking about instead.

I said, "I think you are hoping we will talk about what is important to you and get to the real issues, not just the surface stuff. You want me to notice you and not dismiss you." He replied, "Yes. I want to know why I have always felt this way. I feel like there is something missing, something fundamentally wrong with me."

When Paul was not being distant with me through the robotic, impatient, and often entitled method of relating, he was able to share his anxiety and despair. But it was in a manner that felt overwhelming and fragmented, giving me a taste of what he experienced internally. So, he would zigzag from telling me about people on the street "noticing" him and judging him, to tales about "clinging to my girl-friend's body like a small child desperate for comfort." He would then switch to stories about how ignorant his art teacher was and how he knew so much more about everything in comparison. Paul told me he felt he might be the next star in the world of literature and he could tell how his latest short story for a class left his teacher awestruck. However, Paul also told me he felt sexually weak and impotent and how he "feels devastated when my girlfriend looks away from me during sex. I can tell she has left me, forgotten me!" He cried at this point.

This terrible sense of being forgotten was repeated in the transference when Paul would be talking and then say, "I don't know what I am saying. I am sure it doesn't make any sense to you, only fragments of nonsense. I don't know what I am saying anymore and we are not on the same page. I apologize. I am sorry."

I told Paul that I was easily able to follow what he was saying but he was worried that he created a scramble in our contact and severed our time together. I told Paul he was the one who was perhaps retreating from me after exposing himself too much. He associated to his mother and told me,

> That is exactly what happens with my mother. She only acts like she is interested in me but then turns away and walks out. I know it is because she is anxious and doesn't know how to be with me or anyone, but I feel like I have never been good enough for her to love.

Once again, he began crying at this point. Paul describes his father as also unavailable but for other reasons. He sees his father as very "robotic." Paul's father is an accountant, and Paul says, "He talks to me like one all the time, "never spontaneous or real." So it was interesting that in the transference, Paul had a very difficult if not impossible time being spontaneous and genuine with me from moment to moment.

During a recent session, he had been listening to music in the waiting room through his headphones. He came in and told me he had nothing to say but thought we should continue from where we left off. "I left very sad and crying but I can't remember why. But, it is probably productive to return to that discussion. We will be working on our goals." I asked him why he wanted to be so productive. He told me, "my time here is short and I need to make progress. I should have a topic so we can work on it and make progress." I said,

You seem so demanding of progress and immediate work that it is unclear what you are even working on. You are very anxious to proceed but you won't allow us to relax enough to find out what is wrong and where to proceed. You don't trust that if we were relaxed and you just talked about whatever you wanted that we might learn something.

He replied, "Oh! If I am supposed to do that, I will start right away. I will make sure to relax and talk about whatever I can!" I interpreted that he was now relating to me like a robot ready to take orders.

Paul said, "I think I was distracted by my music so I didn't think of anything to talk about." I asked Paul if he was relaxed and enjoying the music without the usual self-hatred or self-questioning in his mind. He said yes. I said it was interesting how he allowed himself to have fun and enjoy the music without deciding he was bad in some way. Paul said, "Well, it was bad since it distracted me from thinking of a productive topic!" I replied,

You are quick to twist it into something bad that you did. Maybe it is uncomfortable to realize you trust me enough to relax in the waiting room and enjoy some music. We have been productive that way. Normally, you would not allow for that. But, to let in that positive connection between us and between you and the music is uncomfortable so you say it is all unproductive instead.

Paul thought about this for a moment and agreed that it felt right.

But, shortly after, he said, "If that is what I am doing to make myself unhappy and anxious, what do I need to do to stop it?" This was not said with any curiosity or interest, merely a request for an immediate formula or quick cure. I said, "You are not curious about it, you just want to mechanically replace it." He said, "Should I be curious? I can do that!" So, now Paul was going to be mechanically curious to make progress. I said, "When I try and relate to you in a spontaneous way and invite you to do the same, you pull back and become controlled and mechanical, much like you describe your father and mother." This was a transference interpretation of the projective element of his object-relational phantasy.

Paul said,

I see. My father is just a machine, he can't help it but it is very irritating and awkward. My mother is so caught up in her own anxiety and nervous thoughts she turns away from me when I try and express myself. I feel like she doesn't want me and has never wanted me. Something is missing. I don't know what it is, but something is missing.

He began to cry.

This transference of robotic control emerged many times. Paul turned our relational connection, our mutual interest and spontaneous efforts at understanding things, into lifeless, mechanical components of a formula for perfection. Thus, when I mentioned that he seemed to become lost in a loop of certainty and demand, he started telling me he "was now aware of the loop of certainty and was making progress in avoiding the loop of certainty." So I interpreted that Paul was turning us into lifeless machines that needed to go to the repair shop for an upgrade or replacement.

There were also ways in the transference in which Paul pulled me into his more grandiose phantasies which were defensive narcissistic methods of avoiding devastating meaningless or feared abandonment. In the counter-transference, I noticed myself adopting several different positions before looking deeper at the transference and regrouping. An example of this was how in the initial five to ten sessions I found myself caught up in Paul's descriptions of his delusions and his psychotic theories in a way that left me drifting into a mutual superiority and defensive distancing.

When Paul explained his theory about how it might be a good thing to be so anxious from a historical perspective, I temporarily forgot that he had been talking about the awful dread he lived with every day and the constant anxiety that made it impossible for him to build any friendships or love life, let alone pursue much of anything in his day-to-day life. Instead, I felt intrigued and enlightened as he told me how early man had benefited from the anxious members of the tribe because they worried about being killed by disease or animals and were always on the lookout for danger. All the other tribe members went about things without ever thinking ahead and were often the victims of random violence or accidents. Thus, the anxious members of the tribe were responsible for being an early warning system. They were smart enough to notice when members of the tribe were sick so that they could heal them before it was too late. Their sensitivity prevented the tribe from being wiped out. Thus, those people who are seen as sick, disturbed, and troubled individuals in today's society were actually the ones who helped the human race survive early on. They were the heroes with superior powers. I noticed myself becoming intrigued with the story and half believing it. It took me a while to realize that Paul had made himself into a historical hero who was superior to others and able to see everyone's flaws instead of feeling like an anxious loser in his present life, a scared man with no power.

I also noticed myself becoming extra spontaneous, humorous, and friendly with Paul. This was not something I did deliberately, but as a result of the interactive and interpersonal pull of his projective identification-based transference (Feldman 2009). While he responded temporarily to my extra engagement, overall he continued to be stiff, withdrawn, and mechanical. I think that through projective identification mechanisms, Paul shaped me into his wished for, spontaneous, and interested object that he craved (Joseph 1987, 1988). But, in doing so, he put his demand, aggression, and highly charged conflict over love, hate, and knowledge of his object into me. Therefore, he felt overwhelmed and uncertain, and kept his distance. In addition, by shaping me into the warm, engaged one, he had to take on the other side of the psychic split: the role of the distant, mechanical one (Joseph 1989).

I interpreted that in these transference moments Paul was getting the very thing he wanted from me, his parents, and others. Yet, in response, he became even more like them. I said he wanted love, trust, and free-flowing interaction but it frightened him and he wasn't ready to participate with me or with others. I said that this might be his contribution to the stiff, cold world he described. He agreed and cited examples of him being that way and how he worried people would see him as the "quiet cold one." But he was equally worried that if he was to offer his thoughts without any censor, others would see him as an "uptight narcissist who knows more than everyone else."

In the transference, Paul seems to use evocatory projective identification dynamics (Spillius 1988) in which he relates to me in a way that produces particular counter-transference affects (Waska 2005, 2011a, 2011b). Specifically, he seems to use me and locate me in his mind as the wished-for version of mother and father who is spontaneous, curious, and caring. But then, in an acquisitive projective identification move (Britton 1998), Paul became the cold, mechanical parent and left me feeling alone and without an understanding partner. Then, I was the extinguished flame, formally full of life but now feeling dismissed and ignored, almost wrong in my spontaneity.

Over the course of the two months I have met with Paul, he has told me much about his mother. From the specific ways he portrays her, I often found myself drifting in the counter-transference towards particular experiences. For a while, I was picturing her as a very pathological figure in his life. Listening over and over again to Paul's descriptions of his mother's controlling, distant, and self-absorbed ways as well as his experience of feeling almost being loved and noticed by her only to feel dropped and dismissed without any value made me start to recall papers written in the 1960s about the schizophrenigenic mother, who would interact or not interact in ways that left the child completely confused, hated, and broken. I also began to think about the concept of rejecting containers and the no-trespassing, locked-door nature of some more disturbed mothers who will not allow for a healthy projective identification interaction with their child, leading to severe states of dread and psychological fragmentation.

However, I was able to catch myself in this mental enactment (Steiner 2000, 2006, 2011) of Paul's primitive experience of rejection and isolation. I was able to realize that what was missing from my counter-transference musings was Paul's contribution to this mother/child profile. Then, I began to think about the way he withdrew from me, the way he demanded immediate but superficial nourishment from me, and the flip-flop transference in which he was wanting love and spontaneous relating but when he had it he withdrew. I made interpretations about his contributions to the uncomfortable and awkward way he felt with his parents, his friends, me, and strangers. The "something missing" was a two-way street.

Paul was able to take this in and agreed. He told me,

> I can be as mechanical as my father and I think I don't approach my mother very often either. I don't want to go through it all again and I think it is stupid as well. My parents tell me I can be selfish and rude. Probably, I could try harder to get along and talk with them but I get caught up in all these thoughts about what I am doing wrong and what I need to do next.

In telling me about his mother and his upbringing, Paul explained that his mother seemed to always see him as the best at everything regardless of what his ability actually was. She would tell all her friends how smart he was, what awards he had won, and how much better he was than his peers. Paul told me that it "wasn't ever realistic. It was like I was the smartest person on the planet and she was my audience." I interpreted, "But I think what you are trying to tell me is that it didn't feel personal or genuine. She wasn't proud of your actual accomplishments, she was seeing you as this superhero and missing out on the good things about her son." Paul looked sad and nodded yes.

Over the next few sessions, I found opportunities to interpret how Paul had taken on that superhero role and now is convinced he is indeed better than most people. He feels superior and above others. When he told me his theories about how in early civilization man stayed in large packs and would not easily stray from the pack or interact with other packs, it was after he told me how he had been with a group of friends at a park. One of his friends saw another group of friends and suggested they all "hang out" and socialize. Paul became very anxious and left. I told him he was trying to show me how normal he was and that his exit was simply a part of evolutionary patterns. But this was a way to hide how scared he was, how he felt he wasn't enough, and that no one would like him if they got to know him. He said, "I try and stay quiet and still and hope they don't start to think bad things about me. But, maybe that makes me look withdrawn and superior." This was an important moment of reflection about the way he was contributing to his paranoid phantasies.

I also interpreted that given how special his mother believes he is, but not really noticing the real Paul, Paul feels he has to discard his real self and try to live up to this special superhero status for his mother. On the one hand, he enjoyed his superior, perfect bond with his adoring mother in which he could feel above all of humanity. Yet the level of expectation is so rigid and demanding that he feels he is always failing. So, Paul is always on the lookout for ways in which he might be failing and finds plenty of them, as the superhero is a perfect and exacting role. I think that when Paul describes his mother walking out on him, or his girlfriend turning away from him, or me not understanding him, he feels that others are disappointed and judging him as failing to be the star they want. Paul is now haunted by the phantasy of being the star that fails to shine, always letting his mother and everyone else down. With this eternal flaw, he is easily singled out by all as the one who has done wrong, we all look down on him, and he loses the love he craves. He is left desperate and hungry for love and acceptance, clinging to his object but avoiding everyone at the same time. The world becomes a place of superior and inferior creatures who can never relate to, understand, or depend upon each other.

Discussion

In working in the initial stages of the total transference (Joseph 1985) and the complete counter-transference (Waska 2010c, 2011b), we attempt to translate the mysterious and unbearable into something emotionally known and eventually tolerable. Through our counter-transference containment (Mawson 2011; Steiner 1996) and interpretive process, we take the patient's frightening external "not me" experience and help them to shift into a manageable internal state of mind that they are willing to acknowledge, own, and live within.

In the counter-transference, we seek to learn about the projective identification communication process and its impact upon us as a way to gradually contain, translate, and share the burden of growth, difference, and revision of core beliefs (Britton 1998) about self and other. We listen and watch for our patient's reactions to our interpretations and how they seem to use us, place us in their mindscape, and how we become part of their pathological retreat (Steiner 1993, 2011) system. We begin to understand the dangers (Waska 2006) they experience in changing the foundation of their object-relational phantasy world.

During the short time I have spent with Paul, there have been several changes in his external behavior and in his overall anxiety state. He went from smoking pot every day to having not smoked in over a month. He told me he still gets drunk once or twice on the weekends but "is careful about it." He no longer hears himself say frightening things about suicide or threats of a dangerous nature. He seems to be more able to reflect upon himself and consider what I say for a while before transforming it into part of his anxiety-driven system of demand and judgment.

Paul still feels vastly superior as well as cruelly inferior, but he is now also able to consider these internal states as possibly not grounded in reality and therefore within his reach to understand, manage, and change.

Chapter 3

Depressive conflict and the counter-transference experience

Building upon Melanie Klein's (1946) discoveries regarding projective identification, analysts began to examine the clinical value of the analyst's counter-transference when faced with the patient's depressive (Klein 1935, 1940) and paranoid (Klein 1946) anxieties. Bion (1965) noted how the patient manipulates the analyst with determined vigor, operating within the structure of an unconscious internal plan regarding self and object and creating a replica of various familiar conflicts, fears, and desires. Due to the excessive use of projective identification with associated interpersonal and interactive aspects of transference creating a pull, invitation, or seduction process, the analyst is often left operating within a split of his own, feeling either love or hate for the patient and corrupting the analytic quest of knowing or understanding. This makes it difficult to feel confident or clear about subsequent interpretations and thus even easier to succumb to a variety of enactments.

Regarding projective identification, Mawson (2011) sees an important progression of theoretical and clinical work from Bion's ideas to other, more contemporary Kleinians such as Michael Feldman (2004, 2009) and Betty Joseph (1989). Other analysts have discussed similar concepts, including Sandler's (1976) notion of role responsiveness and Leon Grinberg's (1990) papers on projective counter-identification. Grinberg wrote about how some patients are able, through projective identification dynamics, to carry the analyst into various roles and to induce various affects and states of mind.

Britton (1998) has suggested that patients present rigid pathological organizations (Steiner 1987) which comprise unconscious one-dimensional belief systems that prevent compromise and eliminate differences or options. These belief systems come alive in the transference through projective identification. When the patient's interpersonal and interactive acting out carries the analyst into various levels of enactment, the analyst must look to the counter-transference to sort out what his role is in this phantasy (Rosenfeld 1964; Joseph 1989). Once he understands what type of player he has become or is being carried into being, the analyst can gradually translate, through interpretation, the patient's conflict regarding love, hate, and knowledge instead of acting out these unconscious scripts of rigid, ancient, and singular visions of giving, taking, and understanding.

Of course, the analyst must be careful of the possibility that their interpretations are just disguised justifications for more acting out in which the analyst is simply trying to prematurely and aggressively return the patient's projections (Bell 2011). This is similar to what Grinberg (1990) notes about the possible reactions an analyst may have to projective identification, including fighting against it by vindictively forcing the projections back into the patient or passively accepting the projections instead of trying to therapeutically understand, contain, and translate it for the patient.

The following two cases involve transference situations which created a variety of counter-transference experiences. Both patients were primarily struggling with depressive position (Klein 1935, 1940) anxiety and used projective identification as both an evacuative defense as well as a communication device. The case material follows the ongoing clinical issues that arose and how they affected the establishment of analytic contact (Waska 2007, 2010a, 2010b) and the process of working through the patient's core conflicts. In addition, the material will illustrate how the counter-transference was at times a detriment to the analytic process and at other times a vital if not pivotal element of the treatment.

Case material

Don is a patient I have seen for five years in analysis, on the couch twice a week. He is extremely anxious and prone to guilt which leaves him feeling unable to function and perform in the way he thinks he should. Most of this sense of inadequacy is centered around relationships and specifically in sexual relationships. Don's history involves being raised in a religious family with an emphasis on morals, the duty to do the right thing, and the need to please people. Pleasing others and certainly never hurting others was an unconscious duty embedded in Don's mind and then greatly enhanced by a series of external events in his early life. The main one was Don's mother's severe depression and hospitalization which my patient still feels he may have caused by being too reckless in his emotions and behaviors. Furthermore, when Don was not worried about causing her depression, he certainly felt the duty to prevent her from becoming so depressed again. He had to somehow keep her happy. Don's younger brother was killed in an unfortunate car accident in which he was taking the family car for a joy-ride. Don's mother was devastated.

Years later, my patient went joy-riding and almost had the same situation occur. While my patient was not injured, it certainly shook his mother up again and made Don feel very guilty. As a child and teen, there were other situations in which Don felt he was on the verge of causing great chaos and destruction, including buying beer for someone who later had a fatal drunk-driving accident. It was probably a suicide and nothing to do with Don, but he felt it was his responsibility. Another time, my patient accidentally set an area on fire when playing with matches and it went out of control. It was put out just in time but, to this day, Don fears that he could have caused a fatal tragedy for the many people living nearby. So, these are the kinds of things that still plague him.

In his relationships, Don usually feels he is not good enough, not strong enough, and not manly enough. He is sure he will displease or disappoint the girl sexually. When this anxiety reaches a certain level, Don turns the tables and starts feeling that the girl is not attractive or smart enough. He feels bored with her and wants to move on to someone better. Then, Don feels back in control. This superior/inferior dynamic is played out most of the time with romantic relationships and to a lesser or more subtle degree with his other relationships.

In the transference, Don tends to be very docile and compliant but he also presents himself as an intellectual superior thinker. I have to point out how he is taking that stand and to be the voice of reality, but this plays out my role as the one who puts Don in his place or throws cold water on his aspirations and bravado.

In the sexual realm, Don feels he can never perform long enough or hard enough, and his intense anxiety about this leads to failing in exactly those ways. Alternatively, he will withdraw from the relationship out of fear of failing.

So, for years we have been working on these issues and Don has gone from having a casual relationship with someone who had a severe drug problem and who simply used Don to rescue them out of bad situations, to gradually dating healthier women, with better and better results. Most recently, due to our consistent steady work on these issues, Don is dating someone with whom he seems to get along quite well and so far they are enjoying each other's company.

However, Don has imagined several situations where he felt he was sexually failing and not good enough. He was extremely anxious and overwhelmed with panic but challenged himself by staying in the situation instead of retreating. As a result, he did better each time.

The session that I am going to be highlighting was one that followed several sessions in which he was giving me a vivid description of the ways he was making out with this new girlfriend sexually, the exact details of each date, how far they had gone, to what extent they undressed, what they did with each other, and so forth.

In the most recent session, Don was telling me how he had not been able to perform as he wanted and was worried that he was starting to disappoint her. He talked more and more about the "big day" when they would hopefully have intercourse and how he was very worried about how it would turn out. Don told me about the steamy time they had both had the night before, but emphasized how they had not yet made it "to the testing ground" and how that "final moment" might be a big failure.

So, I interpreted:

> You have been sharing extremely sexy material with me but then completely defacing it and stripping it of any sexual value or feeling. You are reducing it to an intellectualized scoreboard in which you feel none of it really

counted because it wasn't the wild lusty dirty event that you pictured you should experience. You were not performing like the stud you should be.

The last part was a reference to how Don felt he should perform like a porn star with girls or they would find him boring and leave.

Another transference track in this session was how Don told me this girl wasn't really up to snuff in his expectations. Her body "wasn't the right body" and they had not yet done anything that he considered "proof that they had a lustful relationship." This had to do with the other phantasy he entertained of wanting a porn star girl so that he could feel proud and manly. Since his new girlfriend did not meet this criterion, Don wasn't sure if he was turned on by her or whether he even liked her any more.

In the counter-transference I felt a combination of feelings. I was used to this aggression/guilt and superior/inferior seesaw Don was putting us on. In addition, I felt he was losing out once again on having a girlfriend because of his inability to live in reality and deal with his anxieties. I felt he would ruin this relationship just as he had messed up the other ones. It seemed as though he had probably finally found someone he could be with but now he would lose her given how he was treating her and thinking of her.

I also thought that Don was acting very superior and looking down on this person. In the transference, he was being arrogant and dismissive of his objects and wanting me to go along with it. But I also felt compassion for Don, since it seemed like if he wasn't acting superior and so intellectual he would feel terrified about ever being good enough to be loved.

So, I ended up interpreting all of this by saying that while the last three or four sessions were highly sexualized reports of all these very sexualized dates with lots of lusty activities just like he always hoped for, he had completely devalued those dreams and was trying to tell me they had no meaning for him whatsoever. I said that he was after this special porn star experience and without that he and the girl were nothing. In addition, he wanted me to see him as the hard stud and porn star as well. I said he has nothing in the end because he can never obtain those expectations of grandeur. He is either failing to produce this special experience he feels we all want from him or she is is failing to please him in that porn star way. So, everybody loses. I interpreted that with me he ends up having nothing good to report, only failures, so we are losers too.

Don thought about this and agreed with me. He then ended up telling me that in fact he had felt very proud and strong on this last date. After a previous date he had felt guilty about having been so turned on that he almost ejaculated in his pants. Don was convinced the girl would be outraged at his "lack of control." Don told me that on the date he had just had the night before this session, he "let himself get turned on and went for it." He did ejaculate in his pants and was surprised that she was okay with that. She didn't feel like he "was too pushy, gross, or pathetic." Don said he was very glad about the way it had all gone. I said that obviously he had found her to be very pretty and alluring since he was so turned on, and suddenly with me he allowed himself to be a normal person having a really good time sharing lusty tales of victory. He nodded with a smile.

So, by paying careful attention to the transference and the counter-transference that resulted, I had a better idea of exactly how Don was viewing me as an object and how he thought his objects needed to be. This was a projection of his own conflicts with love and aggression that were played out in the projective identification field. By interpreting elements of my counter-transference experience, I was able to focus our attention on his unconscious phantasies and anxieties. As a result, I was able to make more accurate interpretations that better illuminated his realm of internal fear and guilt. This led to gradual insight and change.

Case material

Jane is a fifty-year-old patient whom I have been seeing for five years in analytic treatment. During that time she has worked through many issues regarding her parents, her upbringing, and her sense of herself as essentially unlovable. She fears that others do not want her. Jane sees others as potentially harmful in that we can all easily reject her without warning. These phantasies of sudden betrayal and loss have derailed and damaged her ability to make healthy connections, especially romantic ones.

We have worked on the ways in which Jane both protects herself from this loss as well as how she creates the very thing she dreads. One way in which she creates a protective barrier that also results in painful distance and rejection is by talking in very detached ways that are hard to follow. During the transference, Jane uses emotional distance, vague language, and broken speech patterns that trigger me to ask a lot of questions. In the counter-transference, I feel frustrated and begin to grill her for clarification. Sometimes she becomes irritated with me for this. In general, we are left confused and apart.

In the counter-transference I have the distinct feeling of trying to get into Jane's mind but being kept out, with resulting confusion and lack of connection. After a while I feel as if I am pestering her but I am still frustrated, annoyed, and want to demand that she deliver more and be more open with me. From what Jane has told me of her early family experiences, I believe these are all ways that she felt growing up and now still feels. Jane puts this into me through projective identification. Her conflicts and ways of experiencing her objects are being transmitted to me as both a communication and an evacuation of unwanted feelings and memories. Jane's broken, fragmented, and unlinked manner of communicating with me is a projective identification vehicle with which she puts a piece of her present and her past into me for a variety of reasons that we have discovered and worked on over the years.

In experiencing this type of transference with Jane over countless sessions, I have been able to utilize my counter-transference reactions more effectively so that I act out much less, and instead am able to provide more transformative interpretations. On her side, Jane seems to be taking them in more and presenting less broken communication and less acting out. In that sense, we both seem to be changing together in this analytic process.

One example of how her pathological projective identification dynamic continues, although in lessened form, occurred recently when Jane walked into my office and announced: "I will be going to see my friends next week instead of working." That was all she said and then she sat down in silence. This is a very familiar way in which Jane begins the transference encounter. I am left feeling like I don't know what she's talking about. I feel left out, irritated, and want to pester her with questions. In the past, I have pointed out the teasing and rationing manner in which she is relating to me.

Clearly irritated once again, I said, "And what does that have to do with us?" There was a degree of frustration inside of me and possibly in my tone but the essence of what I said was an interpretation about us and how we were being ignored by her statement. Jane paused and said that it just means she's not going to be in town so we won't meet over the next week.

She immediately started talking about where she was going to visit and how she was happy to go see her friends, as she was feeling a bit down. Jane went on to talk in depth about her grief, sorrow, and pain when looking around and seeing that most people of her age "have one or two babies and a husband. I have no babies and no husband." Jane started crying and told me she feels very alone in the world and cheated. This led her to talk about her upbringing with her angry alcoholic father whom she was never able to get close to and her mother who was constantly depressed. Her mother killed herself when Jane was twenty years of age.

All of this seemed to have come to a head a few days prior on Mother's Day. Jane felt devastated to be without a mother now and also thought back to how she felt without a mother as a child because her mother was so unavailable emotionally. At that point in the session, Jane was very shaken and crying. I said I thought her remark about going to see friends with no comment about us was related. I was able to interpret how she made us seem meaningless, unimportant, and something that wasn't even worth mentioning. I said that perhaps this was her angry way of demonstrating how she is unhappy with the lack of closeness in her life. I said that it's very hard for her to miss me and to talk about the value of us, or to place importance on us in a conscious way. Instead, she throws us away because our relationship makes her acutely aware of the pain of loss, the threat of loss, these awful memories of grief and resentment with her family, and the current lack of a family of her own.

Jane agreed and was able to talk at length about how it is hard for her to be open about her closeness with me. She said that her last boyfriend told her the very same thing before they broke up. He told her she seemed cold, distant, and hard to relate to. During the course of their relationship, he had brought it up several times and asked her to be more forthcoming. Jane was able to talk about how she may at times be that way with me as well.

At this point, Jane was crying a great deal and reached down to the Kleenex box for a tissue. She said, "it's empty." In the counter-transference, I noted she rationed her communication to this factual statement, devoid of feeling or emotional significance. In other words, Jane could not ask me for another Kleenex. If she did, she would be too dependent upon me. Since she was so overwhelmed at this point I felt it better to simply notice that idea. I kept it is a part of my counter-transference map or list of clues and information I tried to maintain in my mind.

I got up to get another box of Kleenex for Jane and I took away the empty one to discard it. In my office, there is a large three-foot-high, two-foot-wide ornate ceramic pot sitting on the floor next to my chair. It is a very decorative and beautiful piece of art. Over the years I've also used it as my trash can. I have a liner in it and I put Kleenex, empty bottles of water, and paper into it. Most patients cannot see the inside of the pot from their vantage point, so they only see it as a work of art sitting on the floor of my office.

Over the years, Jane has pointed to the pot and used it as a symbolic prop in her discussions about the dilemmas, crises, and problems she is experiencing. Sometimes I have joined her, and together we use the pot as a symbol in our talks. So, we might be talking about a drama she has created at work with another co-worker and how she "is stirring the pot," how she has dropped herself "into the pot," how it is hard for her to walk away from a bad relationship/pot and find her own good pot, and so forth. Thus, over time, the pot has served a great usefulness in this symbolic way. Many references to the pot have also been about how Jane is always adding so many degrees of personal meaning to events in her life, usually bad ones, and how she's taken reality, put it in the pot, and distorted it into something much bigger and worse. We talk about how Jane cooks up things in the pot that are much bigger and worse than ordinary, how she changes things in the pot away from reality, and how she has put her life in the pot of distorted hopes and dread instead of living it for what it is and facing the sometimes painful reality of life.

When I walked over to the pot with the empty box of Kleenex, crushed it in my hand, and threw it into the pot, Jane sat there looking completely shocked. After a moment of stunned silence, she said, "the pot is only a trash can?" In a rare moment of mutual "ah-ha," I looked at her and said, "Yes. The pot is only a trash can." We both laughed about this sudden breakthrough of insight and moment of shared experience.

We both realized once again, only this time in such a vividly externalized manner, that Jane was constantly dressing up her disappointing container object to be something better, only to soon be disappointed by the reality of it all. Suddenly, she realized that her method of creating an idealized container object is really just a waste, a pot where she throws away her pain, disappointment, and anger, only to have it reappear as a weak and unavailable object that hurts her one more time. In this spontaneous moment in our session, she once again realized how she can and must turn away, let go, and seek out or build a new, more welcoming container that is not just beautiful on the outside but full of garbage on the inside, but a real-world, never perfect container of goodness, balance, and safety.

Discussion

One of the deeper and ongoing issues that colors and confounds the efforts of the analyst to utilize counter-transference as a helpful analytic instrument is that of the patient's relationship to learning, knowledge, and thinking. Love, hate, and knowledge have been classified by Kleinians as three of the bedrock areas of important psychic growth as well as critical psychic conflict (Spillius *et al.*, 2011). When the patient is overly anxious or eager in areas of love or hate, union or difference, desire or defense, and need or envy, thinking is often the first victim. Knowledge, thinking, and learning become a defensive retreat, a battle-ground for omnipotent striving, a place of persecutory fragmentation, or a stagnant graveyard of guilt and regret. As a result, the nature of the transference and its projective identification-based elements can easily contaminate, damage, or cloud the analyst's ability to think and learn about the patient.

Bion (1959, 1962a, 196b) described the need of the infant to be able to tolerate frustration and loss. Hopefully, the lack of a good object is thought about and mourned, so that there is something to hold onto mentally. Knowledge forms a bridge between absence and the return of the good object. If this ability is lacking or if some severe conflict with love and hate has damaged this knowledge-based coping mechanism, then there will be a frightening and devastating bad experience of self and other, of the world as an unbearable place of loss, persecution, and collapse. This is the perversion, destruction, or void of the much-needed container experience we all hopefully have early in life. In optimal childhood development, we have the helpful and hopeful experience of the primary object as helpful filter, translator, and protector of thought and feeling. Eventually, the patient comes to trust themselves as the ultimate container, separate and different from the object (Steiner 1996). Through projective identification, this experience of either healthy or unhealthy thinking is often imparted in the transference, at least in part, to the analyst.

With Klein's discovery of projective identification, the transference is seen by Kleinians as an unconscious method of communicating to the analyst, retreating from the analyst, loving the analyst, or attacking the analyst. In addition, Modern Kleinian Therapy (Waska 2011a, 2011b, 2012) includes the technical focus on the interpersonal pressures put upon the analyst during the more intense moments of transference. Thus, the analyst will constantly be affected in the counter-transference, with enactments becoming unavoidable. As a result, the counter-transference is now seen as a valuable and crucial tool with which to better understand the exact nature of the patient's conflict and from which to better construct accurate interpretations.

Life-and-death instincts (Segal 1993) come to bear in the nature and intensity of conflicts that affect the patient's experience of love, hate, and knowledge.

This is Klein's modification of Freud's view of the two sides of the human condition. Modern Kleinian Therapy (Waska 2010b, 2011b) considers the distinct anti-life and anti-growth or change force that seems to take the upper hand in some patients. The death instinct seems to arise most violently in situations of envy, difference, separation, or challenge to enduring pathological organizations (Rosenfeld 1987) and pathological forms of psychic equilibrium (Feldman 2009; Joseph 1988, 1989). Hanna Segal (1993, 1997) has defined it as the individual's reactions to needs. A person can seek satisfaction for their needs and accept and deal with the frustrations and problems that come with those efforts. This is life-affirming action or the actions of the life instinct. This is life promoting and object seeking. Eventually, this leads from concerns about the survival of the self to concerns about the well-being of the other.

The other reaction to needs is the drive to annihilate the self that has needs and to annihilate others and things that represent those needs. Kleinians see envy as a prime aspect of the death instinct and that early external experiences of deprivation and trauma play as great a role as internal, constitutional factors in the ultimate balance between the life-and-death forces.

The patients examined in this chapter had great difficulty learning about themselves before and during analysis, as it meant learning about the reality of their objects and facing the loss of any idealized maternal object. They would have to accept the lack of an available, soothing maternal object upon which they could depend. The desire to know, mixed with pain and anger, is often projected. So, with Don, he felt under the microscope of his girlfriend, always failing. With Jane, she made me be the one who put her under the microscope and demanded answers.

Klein placed the desire to know the object alongside the life-and-death instincts, seeing all three as fundamental in understanding human motivation. The subject is curious, envious, and wanting to understand the workings of the object. This creates a desire to be inside the other to taste, test, share, own, and be the other. In healthy development, this involves a thirst for knowledge, a drive to find out, and a talent to solve problems by learning. The unknown becomes something that fuels growth and exploration.

In unhealthy or pathological states, the unknown is unbearable, envy of the other takes over, and a desperate and aggressive attack is launched to find entry into the object and take what is inside. This can result in claustrophobic phantasies, fears of reprisal, revenge, and retribution, as well as a sense of self as inferior and without. These patients feel that others know all the answers and they are clueless and left out. Anxieties about knowing can cause learning disorders. Aggressive quests to know everything can cause obsessive disorders that require knowing at all times to prevent a feeling of terrible guilt or a threatening fragmentation at being unfixed and uncontained. In treatment, many patients display a resistance or fear of knowing themselves, feel trespassed by our wanting to know about them, and rely on a primitive system of withholding or of projecting what is inside-out to protect themselves from others knowing more about them. This was the case with both Don and Jane.

In working with patients in analytic treatment, we find that certain conflicts, desires, fears, or gratitude are projected into the object with the hope of containment and possibly understanding or detoxification with an eventual returning of the reformed, solved, or translated material to the owner. The maternal container must be open and receptive or the sender feels shut out and alone with unbearable internal anxiety. The basic function of the analyst interpreting is a model of receiving, containing, modifying, translating, and returning that provides the patient with this fundamental infant/mother experience. There are many ways in which this container/contained cycle can fail, be perverted, or put to the test during the patient's early family experiences as well as duplicated in the transference situation.

Both Don and Jane had family events that left them marked with particular sets of phantasies, feelings, and unconscious belief systems. As a result, they relied on projective identification and splitting to cope with many unbearable anxieties, grief, guilt, and other, often persecutory convictions.

When projective identification is the predominant or exclusive ingredient in the transference, the analyst is often pulled into a variety of roles (Sandler 1976; Joseph 1989; Waska 2004, 2005, 2006) or myriad characters in the patient's internal phantasy life. This invitation, seduction, or kidnap (Waska 2012) occurs in sometimes subtle form and sometimes in a very blatant form. This unconscious phantasy interaction comes alive and takes place interpersonally in the moment-to-moment clinical encounter. Some difficulties arise with patients who are intrusive to the analyst with their projections but demand a no-trespass policy (Williams 2013) in return. They refuse admission into their mind but demand that the analyst function as an on-command emotional flop house.

Spillius et al. (2011) have noted that Bion's concept of the container/contained allows us to understand how projective identification changes the way in which the receptacle behaves and responds. In the counter-transference, Don and Jane carried me into their experiences by enlisting me and locating me into their mind in particular ways. I tried to use the counter-transference as an emotional map to find my way in the confusing moments of darkness and turmoil that emerged in the therapeutic relationship.

Evacuative actions bring out responses in the object. The power of the inner world shapes the external as well as the internal of the other. If the analyst simply responds with enactments, the patient has created a status quo feedback loop in which knowledge and change are prevented. The death instinct prevails, with life, learning, and difference as the victims.

However, if the analyst can notice, contain, modify, and translate the patient's phantasy projections, then there is an opportunity for gradual disconfirmation of the patient's anxiety and phantasy conviction, leading to gradual transformation. Careful monitoring of the counter-transference can be a valuable part of the ongoing quest for analytic balance, clarity, and transformation.

Part II

Counter-transference elements of modern Kleinian psychoanalytic work

Chapter 4

Pushed to the limits in the counter-transference

Formulated by Klein in her now classic 1946 paper, projective identification is an unconscious phantasy in which aspects of the self or internal object are attributed to another internal or external object. These phantasies may be either positive or negative in nature and may or may not have interpersonal aspects to them that engage others in patterns which confirm the patient's core phantasy conviction (Joseph 1985, 1989; Gabbard 2004). Besides attributing aspects of the self to another, projective identification can also involve communication of unspeakable or unknown feelings, the desire to help or be helped, of control and fighting off control, or of acquiring and owning aspects of the other (Feldman 2009). Thus, the motives of projective identification are many and can be part of healthy normal development and relating, or be part of destructive, defensive pathology (Rosenfeld 1983, 1987; Waska 2004, 2006, 2010a).

To truly work effectively, we must be and always are unavoidably immersed within the patient's projective identification phantasies to some degree, whether within the interpersonal matrix, the intra-psychic level, or both (Feldman 1994, 2008; Joseph 1987). It is as if there is a shower running overhead at all times. We cannot ever step out of the shower to dry off and to clearly reflect upon the clinical encounter. The water is running all the time. So, we must try to think while soaking wet. Sometimes we're able to adjust the volume of water and sometimes we can adjust the temperature; but we are always wet.

Thus we have some control and some degree of coping and operating in that constantly changing transference environment, but we are never fully removed from the counter-transference immersion process. We strive to help the patient develop an as-if way of thinking instead of acting out what they believe to be reality, unaware that it is a product of unconscious conflict and phantasy. In the counter-transference we struggle with the same thinking. It is important in the counter-transference to be aware that our feelings may also be part of a phantasy or conflict and in keeping that in mind we hopefully don't act out as much.

This is connected to the importance of how we interpret. Whenever we interpret, we must monitor our counter-transference so that we can effectively interpret in a less contaminated fashion. We must leave open the possibility that efforts towards and away from love, hate, or knowledge in the transference are a defense or distortion, or at least not a complete reality. We must always convey our conviction of this in the interpretation. However, if we are too caught up in the counter-transference our interpretation will convey our belief that problems with love, hate, and knowledge are real and something to react to just as strongly and just as out of control as the patient does. This only serves to convince the patient that their deepest fears are true and then we both slip deeper into the darkness of their paranoid and depressive (Klein 1935, 1940) anxieties.

In exploring the nuances of counter-transference, I believe that all analysts are constantly contributing to the transference anxieties that the patient experiences to some degree. In other words, whatever the particular anxiety, phantasy, or unconscious conflict the patient has, there is going to be something that the analyst will do, say, or be that will contribute to the validation of the patient's fears, desires, and conflicts. We cannot help but have certain aspects of our personality that are less than perfect, no matter how much analysis we have gone through or how much we continue to monitor ourselves in the counter-transference.

Certain pieces of our personality are more jagged and unpolished than others and will provide a landing area for certain patients who are unconsciously looking for that particular match or mismatch. This clinical dilemma arises much more with chaotic, challenging, and disturbing patients who create a great deal of confusion and tension in the transference that more readily exposes those jagged and unpolished areas of our personality.

In this sense, every analyst has some type of emotional "kindling" that they will be adding to the analytic encounter. This kindling has the potential to start a transference fire, but it is only a potential that may or may not be eventually realized. It depends on the intensity of the kindling and how the patient uses or reacts to it. If the analyst is undergoing some sort of personal crisis, or some type of unworked pathology is surfacing for some reason, they may have much more emotional kindling and as a result they may be really helping the patient to build a fire. This is more of a genuine counter-transference pathology than the more usual and expectable counter-transference reaction most analysts may have to a given transference situation.

We know that every analyst will have a small amount of kindling but if they know that about themselves and try to consider it in the clinical situation, things will be bumpy on occasion but overall the counter-transference will not be a hindrance to the patient's recovery process.

However, intense moments between analyst and patient may result in dramatic states of counter-transference that block effective therapeutic working through or healing, and possibly reinforce existing pathology. Borderline or narcissistic patients quickly establish and escalate conflict in the therapeutic relationship and corrupt the analyst's ability to provide a defining, translating container such patients sorely need to modify and integrate their pathological patterns of projective identification (Feldman 1992; Rosenfeld 1979; Waska 2002, 2005).

Chaotic moments with two patients are examined to provide insight into the potential benefits of using counter-transference as part of working with such turbulent patients. This case material will also highlight the ongoing pitfalls and potholes that naturally occur in the counter-transference when faced with such insatiable and unrelenting aggression, envy, and rigidity.

Case material

I am a provider for what's called EAP services. An employee is given three free sessions from their company to see a mental health worker. This is for a brief assessment and possible referral. After almost thirty years, I have found that it is fairly common for the more disturbed narcissistic or borderline patient to use this service as a free pass to imagined instant and painless relief that they feel entitled to and don't have to work for. After the free sessions, they seldom continue because they would have to pay some amount themselves. They simply want to take. They feel entitled to some sort of magical solution from the three visits.

Now, certainly some people use those free sessions in a very healthy way, show genuine motivation, and make as much progress as anyone could in three visits, but it isn't surprising when it goes the other way.

So, I received a phone call from a woman who said that she was a nursing intern at a hospital and had been there for a year. She said they had "promised" her a full-time position when her internship was completed but that it was never "in writing." She told me she'd been promised this job and a year had gone by, but they did not give her the job. She was "devastated and couldn't believe that they had gone back on what they said." She couldn't believe they had "done this to her" and that she wanted to sit down and talk to someone about it. She said she knew she "had these free sessions and wanted to use them to talk about these terrible events."

Some feelings and thoughts came up in the counter-transference as I listened to my voicemail. The first thing was that my voicemail message starts with "Hello, you have reached the offices of Dr. Robert Waska." Ninety-nine percent of the time when a new patient leaves a message, they say, "I'm calling for Dr. Waska." Every once in a while – and I have a distinct counter-transference sensation each time it happens – a patient will leave the message "Hello Robert."

When this happens, I am almost always struck by how it sounds as if they are trying to devalue me, to make sure I feel they are in control, that they are immediate equals or peers, or that they get to be pseudo-close without earning it or without permission. So, in the counter-transference, it feels like an invasion, an insult, or both. While it could certainly be a way of trying to be close without any aggressive motivation, I have yet to see that once I meet them, if indeed they ever actually make it to the first appointment.

Most of the time, when I do meet such a patient and begin a treatment process, they quickly impress me as a borderline or narcissistic individual who is rebelling against my authority, putting me in my place, and turning the tables to make sure they never feel inferior or dependent. So, since most people initially call me Dr. Waska at least until we have met in person and establish a relationship, I considered this voicemail message the first red flag.

The second red flag was that this woman felt very angry at the hospital because she felt she was "promised" something. She had said it in a way that made me think she felt entitled to "the promise" and now she feels it has been yanked away from her. Her story may be the true situation of what had happened but the manner in which she relayed it made me suspicious. It made me also wonder if she was a problem at the hospital and that therefore she wasn't given the job. Now, perhaps, she is going to use the free EAP services to complain about the hospital and maybe cause them trouble. Sometimes, patients in such situations have wanted me to validate their complaints and fill out legal papers to sue the hospital or demand some type of disability compensation. So, I wondered if I was going to be used in that fashion.

I was aware of these feelings in myself and tried to not act on them in any fashion. However, I must be open to the idea that when I called her back some of my feelings may have sprung out in some manner. This is what I call counter-transference "kindling." It can provide certain patients with a landing zone in their search or hunt for expected self–object matches and mismatches. If there is no kindling available, they will do their best to create it through the interactive and interpersonal aspects of projective identification.

What this particular person on the phone did with the kindling, if there was any, was dramatic and diagnostic.

Depending on how rushed I may be that day, how complicated the patient's EAP or insurance coverage is, or what type of logistical problems I encounter with the referral, when I make the initial phone contact with a new patient I will sometimes say, "it sounds like there's a lot going on for you. Let's figure out how we can meet and talk about it." With other patients, I may simply ask them what office they want to meet in, suggest a time to meet, and set up the appointment. If I feel there is a great deal of potential acting out or transference power struggle already in play, I may choose to set some limits. I establish a simple but defined frame by keeping the initial phone contact to something very basic and only about appointment times. That was the case with this patient.

I felt she was presenting something in her message that sounded provocative or charged in some way. I did not want to fuel that or become involved over the phone without ever having met her. So, I elected to stick with simply setting up the appointment. However, I may have decided upon those ways of interacting because of some counter-transference reaction. In other words, my way of responding to her may have been some form of counter-transference kindling from the initial therapeutic immersion process.

I may have been reacting to her calling me Robert in what sounded to me like a disrespectful tone. So, perhaps I was trying to get back at her by being very simple and straightforward in my relating on the phone. When I called her back and she answered, I said, "Hello. This is Dr. Waska. I got your message. I do have some time to meet with you, but I'm wondering which office you would like to meet at?" She told me which one and I said okay. Then I said, "When you mentioned you wanted to use the EAP service, have they given you an authorization number yet?" I always ask this of all patients because that is the procedure with EAP services. The authorization must be in place and then paperwork is sent to me. Without that in place, the treatment cannot begin. She said she had not asked for an authorization yet because "they have given me three different names of therapists and I want to talk to all three to see which one is the right match for me."

With some patients this makes sense and doesn't raise any red flags. However, there is a way in which some patients engage in this as an entitled free shopping trip they will take until they find someone to cater to them exactly as they wish. I told her that's fine but in order to make an appointment I need the paperwork, and to get the paperwork we need an authorization. So, if she wants to meet we do need to get that in place. She said she had the authorization number but it was "in the other room. I'll have to get up and go get it." She paused and said, "But, I'm busy right now. I'll have to call you back." I thought this was a moment of uncertainty on her part that showed her level of anxiety, but mostly it felt as if it was simply too much of an effort for her to have to go to the other room to get the number. I felt brushed off, like a hassle that she didn't want to bother with. I said, "No problem. Give me a call back when you can."

Two hours later I received a voicemail for "Robert." She was quite angry and told me that I was "an insensitive person." She said I should have listened to what was the matter with her, asked her questions, and tried to empathize with her. She said I should have tried to find out why she was so distraught instead of just directly asking about her insurance. She said I had an "incredibly bad bedside manner" and that I "was obviously not a very good therapist." She "wanted to give me that feedback" and then hung up. This was all said in a very devaluing, insulting, and superior tone.

So, this was a jarring experience but one that unfortunately is not unusual in private practice with the many borderline and narcissistic patients we see who immediately begin relating like this. In thinking about it, I believe the essence of the transference was that she felt somehow entitled to this "promise from her hospital" and wanted things to be done in a certain way. She expected something to be given to her and then felt very disappointed. Her object was now this disappointing bad thing that hurt her and disappointed her.

So, it seems that with me this internal conviction was repeated. I think she felt entitled to a certain amount of promised free EAP loving and understanding from me in a very particular and immediate way. When I didn't deliver, she felt I had broken a promise and was hurting her and disappointing her again.

As I mentioned above, I could have certainly contributed to this problem with my own counter-transference kindling. However, what this patient did with this kindling in this particular clinical situation was unique. Unconsciously, I think she was looking for a specific feeling, circumstance, and meaning to fulfill an internal conviction. She quickly found it with me and immediately used it to fan a destructive psychological Inferno. Many borderline and narcissistic patients are like that. They are looking intensely for a certain type of kindling. Once locating it in our personality or behavior, they will then seize upon it and put a match to it as soon as possible. If they cannot find the kindling they are looking for in the actual flaws or enactments of the analyst, they will convince themselves they see it anyway and act accordingly. Or, through relentless acting out, they will force the analyst to produce their expected kindling, fulfilling their predictions of flames and heat (Joseph 1988; Waska 2010b, 2010c).

Such patients are emotional pyromaniacs who are ready to do battle. In the transference, through pathological reliance upon projective identification mechanisms, they force us to be both persecutory neglecters as well as manipulated firemen trying to put out the flames. Regarding the actual kindling we may be generating, other patients will be more forgiving. They will ignore it, deny it, or will forgive us. They may react to it, but in a minor way. That is more of a depressive position reaction to someone else's flaws and faults as opposed to taking a more paranoid reaction to a fleeting or temporary problem or disappointment as confirmation of being attacked and not being offered the gifts to which one feels entitled.

I am not saying it is healthy for our patients to be in denial if we hurt them. Hopefully, they can move past their own guilt or fear of confronting us. Likewise, we must work past our own guilt, denial, fear, or sense of superiority to acknowledge within ourselves our personal kindling and begin to shift our stance with the patient to a healthier, less distorted method of relating that does not so easily replicate or trigger their fundamental conflicts.

The essence of our therapeutic efforts in the counter-transference is to truly know, to learn about and understand, the nature of the patient's inner world and the elements of their internal conflicts. This is what analysis is all about. To do this, we must become our patient for a while and become their objects to some degree. This is what Racker (1953) meant by complementary and concordant counter-transference states. Just as the patient's ability or inability to find peace of mind and clarity of thought is the result of internal battles between love and hate, these conflicts color the transference in ways that leave us struggling with difficult feelings of love and hate that cloud our ability to think straight.

Bion (1962) and many contemporary Kleinians have used the concept of epistemphia, or the quest for knowledge, as a way to understand the deeper emotional struggles our patients endure or feel overwhelmed by. Bion (1962) has described the container and contained concept as an internal experience linked by love, hate, and knowledge. The resistance to knowledge, the avoidance of learning about the self, is often a great obstacle in treatment. When it is an intense part of the transference, this evading of knowledge about self and other can seep into the counter-transference, with the analyst turning away from knowledge as well.

This scenario may occur in many clinical situations, but it is more common when the transference is difficult to bear and the analyst is under the weight of hard-to-acknowledge, hard-to-tolerate, and hard-to-contain projections.

Case material

An example of the urge to abort knowledge as a therapeutic tool and instead engage in a more hate-focused enactment occurred recently with a new patient. By carefully monitoring my counter-transference, we were able to also make significant headway within the confines of a very difficult and trying clinical climate. Ian was mandated to see me for assessment and brief therapy. He had been accused of sexual harassment and as a result was close to losing his job.

Ian seemed both arrogant and anxious as he sat down in my office. I began the session by asking what he felt had happened that resulted in the mandatory referral. Ian told me a long story about how he had met this woman at work and found her to be quite beautiful. He tried to ask her out many times over the course of the next year. Each time this woman would say, "No thank you." Ian said, "She said it with a smile so I knew she was thinking about saying yes." My impression of the story was that the woman was probably trying to be polite each time and he took it as her being seductive and interested. So he kept asking her out.

On Valentine's Day, Ian gave her a card with a big heart on the front. Inside he wrote that he hoped they could be "special friends." She again said no. Ian kept at it, and each time she told him she did not want to spend time with him. I asked Ian about this and again he said, "She smiled whenever she said no so it obviously meant that she actually did want to go out with me." Ian said he knew she wanted to date him by the way she acted, so he kept pursuing her. He added that "she was flirting with me all the time."

I asked him what he meant. Ian said, "She smiles at me when she talks." I said that he seems to want to feel liked and wants this so much that he sees a smile as an invitation and wants to believe she is interested. Ian said, "Well, I do like to be liked. That is a big thing for me." Then, he continued to tell me about how he didn't see a problem with any of this until he was told by his manager that there was a protest filed and he was told to leave the woman alone or else.

After the woman's protest was filed, Ian said she kept coming into his office area "smiling, flirting, and asking me questions that she didn't really need to be asking. So, it seemed obvious she was still interested." He said, "So, what was I supposed to do? A pretty woman throws herself at me. Of course I will respond." So, I told Ian he seems to be blaming her for all the trouble that's happening and that he's not taking any ownership or accountability.

He said, "Well, maybe. But, she is a beautiful woman and I just can't help myself. That is just the way men are. We can't help it, especially if the woman is pretty. She seems to want me." I brought up the fact that this woman has a boyfriend so why was he being so arrogant to dismiss that obvious limit. Ian said,

"It doesn't matter if a woman has a boyfriend. I don't care. I've worked my way past that before with other women and eventually they will want me instead of their boyfriend." Here, I was amazed at the degree of his narcissistic entitlement and arrogance. In noting my feelings, I was able to gather myself and try to make a helpful interpretation rather than simply lash out in reaction to his pompous stance.

I said, "It's hard for you to realize that you are unwanted sometimes and that there is another man who already has what you want." Ian said, "Absolutely. I don't like that at all. I never have liked that. If I feel that there is a girl I like, I will make sure to get them no matter what it takes." Here, in the counter-transference, my feeling of fear, judgment, and suspiciousness was elevated in my mind. I started thinking, "This is a classic sociopath. This is what a rapist looks like." I noticed these feelings and then tried to contain them because otherwise I would be judgmental of him and put him down in some way.

So, instead, I tried to focus on what might be behind this and I said, "I wonder why it's so hard for you to cope with feeling rejected and why you seem to treat women as commodities, like some kind of property that you can own." Ian said, "Well, they are commodities and that's how I see it." Here again, I felt that my judgmental feelings were confirmed, that Ian was someone who has no sense of ever caring for others. I asked him if he has always felt that way. Ian said, "Yes. I think I get that from my father. He was a real player as well."

I asked Ian what he meant. He went on to describe how his father had a pattern of cheating on his mother throughout their marriage. This produced a child with another woman and eventually Ian's parents divorced when he was ten years old. Ian added that his father was a very "stern man." When I asked about this, he offered details about his father being violent and angry without warning. Ian said, "We did not want to cross him. He was quick to hit with the belt or the belt buckle." Here, I felt more empathy for my patient and began to have a sense of why he might be operating in this very cold and callous way. I made interpretations to this effect and Ian seemed to be able to understand them and take them in for a moment.

However, at the same time, he maintained the idea that women are just there to enjoy and he should not feel bad, since they were obviously seducing him. When he took this macho narcissistic stance, I would immediately establish a very rigid and firm container. I told Ian that this was a way he was abusing or hurting people, and he was being arrogant and selfish in the process. Once this more strict and defined boundary container was established, it seemed that we could return to finding out more about the nature of his mindset in the present as well as its origin in the past. This helped us start to work on some of his preda-tory ways of viewing the object.

I told Ian that he seemed to ignore or despise what most people agree to be the social standards and acceptable limits of behavior, but I tried to make sure that I did not overreach and impose my own personal judgment, morals, or life-style upon him in reaction to any negative counter-transference feelings.

In my counter-transference, I noticed that three areas began to gel in my mind. One feeling was that I simply wanted to put him down. I wanted to tell Ian that he was bad. The second feeling was an awareness of his need for a strict and firm containment. In the counter-transference, it seemed as if Ian was a wild beast, a wild animal that needed to have a pen put around him, a corral to confine him while we worked on taming his dangerous wildness. My third feeling was that we were trying to understand and heal his wildness and that Ian was able to join me momentarily to look at it before deflecting our mutual interest. Although quite uncertain about his motives, I did feel hopeful about finding what was at the core of all these issues.

When we were talking about the sexual harassment allegation, I brought up the fact that after the first warning from his manager to leave the woman alone he went ahead and sent her an email. He said it was "no big deal" and had brought it in for me to read. Essentially, Ian started out by apologizing but then took it back and said that he was very much infatuated with her and wanted to be with her. She brought this email to his boss and this led to a second warning at work. Ian was told to come to my office for several visits or be immediately fired.

When I told Ian that once again he seem not to care about what others were telling him or the limits that were set by the girl and his manager, he said, "Well, if they seemed serious about it and really meant 'no', I might respect that. But obviously she was flirting with me and likes me." So, again, I interpreted that he is so afraid of being rejected that he sees everybody flirting with him all the time. Ian said that could be because he doesn't like to be rejected. He talked a little more about it and so I had the sense that when I made interpretations focused on his narcissistic style of relating offering a firm and defined containment, it did seem to lead to a temporary moment of insight, with Ian lowering his walls of defense. This also occurred when he would lie outright to me about something, and I would say, "You are lying. You are trying to make me see you one way but it is obvious that you are just trying to get your way." He would splutter a bit and then say, "You are right. I am sorry. I see what you mean." And, then, for a few moments, we seemed to be back on a more genuine and productive track.

After the first session, Ian called the EAP office to complain that I never showed up for his sessions. After I talked to them to clarify that I had indeed met with Ian, I spoke to Ian about it during our second session. First, he denied that he had done it at all. I told him he was lying to me and he was making me look bad to the EAP company for some reason. After confronting him several more times about his outright lying, Ian admitted he had done it so he could make sure that his attendance was being reported accurately and his workplace knew he was attending.

I told him,

You are lying to me and manipulating me and the EAP company in order to have control over all of us and make sure you get what you want. You may be worried that I am not taking care of you and then you will get into trouble but what you are doing is lying, causing me trouble to get what you want, and trying to control everyone behind the scenes.

Ian went back and forth but then admitted it and said, "I am sorry. It was a pretty lame way to operate. Now that you explained it like you did, I can see how I mistreated you. I am sorry. I guess I am a pretty bad liar and I can see why you are angry." I thought this was genuine and, as a result of the more thick-skinned narcissistic (Rosenfeld 1987; Waska 2011a, 2011b) confrontation and interpretation, he was able to engage me in a more real moment of self-reflection and take ownership of his effect on the object. At the same time, I also felt that Ian was simply embarrassed at being caught and wished he had been more stealthy about how he manipulated his objects.

When he talked more about how this was the girl's fault and he just wanted to be with her, I reminded him that he wasn't acknowledging the fact that not only did the girl have a boyfriend but that he already had a girlfriend himself throughout most of this incident. Ian responded with a "So what?" In the counter-transference, I once again felt that I was dealing with an evil sociopathic. So, I tried to regain my analytic balance and find meaning in what was happening. I interpreted that when Ian says "So what," he is indicating that he will not tolerate any limits and no disappointment. He wants what he wants when he wants it. In doing so, Ian does not seem to care if he hurts his girlfriend and doesn't want to have the restrictions of having a girlfriend, which would normally mean that he isn't allowed to pursue other girls.

In response, Ian told me that he doesn't really care about his girlfriend, that their relationship is just temporary, and that's how guys are. I said, "So, you just have something to use until you're done with it." He nodded and smiled. So, again in the counter-transference, I felt afraid and disturbed by his way of viewing his objects, but I was also able to reflect upon what type of projective identification effort was taking place and then I told Ian,

> You have a girlfriend so that means you can't do anything else with other girls. That is what that means. So, maybe you don't like to deal with feeling limited and unwanted. Maybe you easily feel alone and rejected as a result of your difficult relationship with your parents and also now in your present life.

Ian agreed and talked about how difficult it was in his family with the violence and his father's erratic behavior.

Then, Ian told me that in fact he had "recently realized" that he "sort of likes his girlfriend and maybe they are a good match after all." He said this was a big surprise to him but he thinks "maybe he might be in for the long haul with her." While these sudden moments of reflection could just be Ian lying to me as part of his ongoing manipulation, I felt he was being genuine for a fleeting moment, almost a different person actually connecting with me and with himself. I think he was able to step out of his pathological organization (Steiner 1990, 1993) for a short period before he slipped back in and slammed the door shut. However, since he talked of his girlfriend as a commodity which he simply used when needed and then said he "sort of likes her" ten minutes later, I do think that if it wasn't lying outright, he was demonstrating the severe splitting that occurs in his mind and the resulting confusion of reality due to a severe lack of mental integration.

So, overall, in the two sessions with this challenging patient, I noticed three zones of counter-transference experience. First, I felt hatred, fear, and judgment. When I was able to step back from that, I realized Ian seemed to need a firm and defined containment to keep him corralled like a wild animal in a structured environment in which I could make emotionally taming observations (Waska 2012) and empathic interpretations. This analytic approach seemed to lead to much more back and forth between us about what was really going on psychologically, both in his past and present internal experience. Once more relaxed or less anxious within this corral of firm containment, Ian was able to internalize my supportive confrontations and interpretations about his need to not be rejected.

I told Ian, "You cannot feel unloved. You won't allow it." In response, he told me more and more about his history with his abusive father who was cheating on his mother all the time and how the divorce was "very hard on us all." In telling me how he ended up feeling like a child, he revealed very vulnerable insights about how he does not allow rejection because he doesn't like the idea of not being wanted.

So, there was this back-and-forth relationship emerging. In the counter-transference, I was reasonably successful in maintaining a stable analytic state in which I wasn't just reacting to him but instead I was gradually organizing and translating what he was putting into me and what he was refusing to own, feel, and expose. In response, Ian was being able to be less defensive and a little more sensitive. In these rare moments, he was beginning to reflect more upon his past and current motivations.

At the same time, it was clear that Ian was not taking full ownership of his actions; he still very much believes that he was not at fault, and he still feels he has the right of ownership to women. He sees himself as superior and above any regular norms or limits. But, after two sessions, there was a dramatic, albeit temporary shift in what initially looked like a very hard-core case of someone who appeared to be predatory, entitled, and emotionally dangerous.

Unfortunately, Ian is only mandated to see me for a total of five sessions. I believe he may be able to significantly change some of his fundamental conflicts if we met for another fifty or a hundred sessions. But that is not how the American health care system works. Ian has let me know that he will be happy when he has completed the five sessions, as he sees our time as "useless and unneeded" but "somewhat helpful and occasionally interesting." He made this latter comment in a condescending manner but I think he may have actually meant it underneath. So, it is sad to see Ian ready to end what could be a long and possibly fruitful journey before it ever gets off the ground. However, this is usually the norm with these types of very complicated and troubled patients.

Discussion

When patients terminate, whether by agreement or by sudden abruptness, the analyst will experience certain resulting depressive or paranoid counter-transference feelings and phantasies. Depending on the nature of the patient's projective identification efforts in the transference, this can mean the difference between the sense of being discarded or abandoned as useless and a sense of sadness and understanding while still feeling frustrated and wishing it didn't happen. There are some narcissistic patients such as Ian who abruptly stop, whether after five sessions or five months, tossing us away with contempt. In the counter-transference, we either have no feeling at all as a defensive move or we have an angry reactive "good riddance" sensation.

Schafer (2002) discusses the difficulties of termination for both patient and analyst and how either or both parties can pretend to cope by falsely adopting a depressive position stance of maturity and understanding. I wish to extend Schafer's ideas beyond the termination phase of analysis to examine certain difficult aspects of counter-transference that occur throughout the entire treatment, especially with the more disturbed patient.

From a diagnostic standpoint, the difference between depressive patients and paranoid patients is often reflected in the counter-transference. We can have a depressive reaction or a paranoid lapse, either of which influences the types of interpretations we make or the way we may relate to the patient. With Ian, I felt a confusing mix of depressive feelings alongside more intense persecutory ones.

The entire enterprise of analytic treatment is really the constant introduction of depressive tasks and hardships such as separation, difference, loss, accountability, give and take, and mourning to both parties. With more difficult and primitive patients, these new ways of being are introduced into a mindset wanting more ideal visions of self and other in which independence, superiority, and never having to lose are often the more familiar realm of experience.

With more depressive patients, the ideas of control, denial of pain or loss, and manic and magical maintenance of idealized visions of self and other are more the norm. For them, fear of conflict, avoidance of individuation, and guilt over desire are common ways of organizing the world.

So, the new ways of viewing and treating the self and other that psychoanalytic treatment offers are painful moments for both patient and analyst to internalize and tolerate, let alone accept. As Schafer (2002) notes, both parties can react defensively by either paranoid-schizoid relating, retreating to pathological organizations and acting out, or by slowly allowing change, dependence, loss, incompleteness, and the lack of complete knowledge about the world.

These issues were a constant factor in the two sessions with Ian, as they are with most hard-to-reach borderline and narcissistic patients. We must find a reliable and sturdy container that serves as a defining, securing, and organizing system for ourselves and for the patient. With patients such as Ian, we must often build a reliable container from scratch in the counter-transference and often on the fly. In addition, it is not uncommon for us to feel as if that container is torn down or burnt to the ground many times over in the treatment process. As a result, we must try to salvage the wreck and rebuild again. Of course, in the process, it is easy to slip and fall in the counter-transference and begin to act out, only verifying the patient's worst fears or most distorted expectations.

In constructing a robust container for ourselves and our patients, we are erecting a temporary shelter or healthy psychological retreat from the unbearable depressive (Klein 1935, 1940) or paranoid-schizoid (Klein 1946) nature of the patient's phantasy and internal unconscious belief system (Britton 1998), which comes to quickly affect the analyst via projective identification. By realizing we are always part of the patient's internal historical experience of self and other, we can use the counter-transference to try and find our way out of the patient's psychological darkness and hopefully eventually lend them our flashlight of insight to show them how we found our way. Then they may choose to do the same.

Chapter 5

Working to understand our role in the patient's mind

Counter-transference and the problems of immersion

In the course of analytic treatment, the analyst experiences many strands of counter-transference conflict which are the result of complex transference dynamics. Projective identification often plays a significant role in their intra-psychic and interpersonal interactions. Due to the intensity of some patients' projective efforts, these counter-transference moments of imbalance include periods of deep immersion within the patient's emotional struggles with love, hate, and knowledge (Bion 1965, 1967) in which desire, aggression, and learning are part of complicated internal battles. In these clinical situations, the analyst is pulled into various enactments and often becomes caught up in a number of specific counter-transference patterns that parallel the patient's unconscious world. When examined closely, these counter-transference struggles and associated acting out are valuable signposts to what the patient is unable to tolerate or emotionally share. Instead, they feel compelled to discard, disguise, or discharge their phantasies and conflicts into the analyst.

As Grinberg (1990) notes, this can be to communicate, to preserve, to repair, to evacuate, to control, or to destroy. I would say this is only a partial list of unconscious motives that underlie projective identification and its foundational role in shaping the transference. Understanding our place in the patient's internal world by gradually making sense and meaning of our counter-transference can lead to helpful interpretations and a reduction of anxiety and acting out for both parties.

As a result of these direct and strong unconscious maneuvers of the patient to either locate themselves in the analyst's mind or to bring the analyst into their mind in some capacity, the analyst may have moments or extended periods of being caught up in a paranoid (Klein 1946) or depressive (Klein 1935, 1940) counter-transference experience. This will shape and direct the analyst's method of interpreting and of relating to the patient. While often unavoidable, this may lead to upheavals in or disruptions of the treatment. If the analyst can become aware of these clinical soft spots, there is a chance for the analyst to grasp some understanding and then attempt to pass that learning on to the patient through interpretations. This is an attempt, while immersed in the projective counter-identification (Grinberg 1990), at decoding what the patient is trying to do with the analyst and to begin to translate that to the patient. We try to find where we are being located in the patient's mind and what role we play in their core phantasy, and we begin to talk about that with the patient instead of simply fulfilling our role in the unconscious historical script.

This process may not always decrease the patient's intense anxiety, continuous acting out, or early termination, difficulties all so common with more borderline or narcissistic patients, but it is a way of possibly conveying the hidden meaning or lost communication to the patient. This can momentarily reduce anxiety and provide a sense of hope or temporary trust which may prevent a complete collapse of the treatment. If we are lucky, it may buy us more time to possibly establish a more secure therapeutic footing.

In order to be the best possible analyst and truly hear the hidden and distorted messages that our patients convey on a conscious, unconscious, and interactive level, we must have an extra sensitivity to how others relate to us interpersonally and psychologically. We must have an ability to understand how the match or mismatch of two parties takes place, including how we contribute to its positive or negative flavor.

This extra sensitivity is crucial for the analyst to have but may also be a liability in certain circumstances. Especially with the more difficult patient who presents a pressing, thorny, and intense transference, our sensitivity may bring us into overwhelming, confusing, or painful states of counter-transference. In some sense, this is unavoidable when working from a deep psychoanalytic perspective. The reality of the clinical situation is that we are always immersed to some degree in the psychological conflict that unfolds in the transference. Through projective identification, we are always pulled into the patient's internal experience of self and other at some level (Gabbard 2004). This may mean we experience what the patient feels or we may step into the role of the patient's object (Racker 1957). Either way, it is rare that we are not in some type of enactment because of what I call the immersion process inherent in the psychoanalytic process.

When the patient's projective identifications shape and color our counter-transference, we enter into close contact with the patient's core unconscious phantasy life. This phantasy life is an internal experience that emerges interpersonally at times, bringing external representation to internal, unconscious object relationships between self and other that underlie all mental processes. These phantasies are the expression of conflicts and defenses surrounding love, hate, and knowledge. These elements of human struggle and desire are what psychoanalytic treatment hopes to bring into more conscious awareness and result in integration.

The immersion process is critical to and unavoidable in the psychoanalytic process. We become very familiar and often identify with the patient's internal objects. Melanie Klein has outlined how throughout life the subject projects their various feelings and thoughts about self and other on to their valued or despised object and then internalizes the combination of reality and their distortion back inside. This starts another cycle of unconscious coping and reaction to that new internal object which is then projected again. Thus, there is a never-ending recycling of one's vision of self and other that one is continuously organizing, relating, and reacting to, both externally and internally, both intra-psychically and interpersonally.

In the paranoid-schizoid position, these internal objects are often fragmented part objects rather than the more integrated whole objects experienced in the depressive position. The paranoid-schizoid position is a more immature, primitive state of mind which Melanie Klein encountered in her patients, a state in which objects and the self are experienced in one-dimensional, black-and-white tones that involve splitting and more rudimentary psychic functioning. This blunted state of mind is dominated by projective identification, splitting, idealization, and devaluation, leaving the subject feeling persecuted and abandoned by bad objects or united with and loved by idealized objects (Hinshelwood 1989).

The paranoid-schizoid mode is usually found in more borderline, narcissistic, or psychotic patients but we all exist within this mode to some degree or can easily regress to it under trying circumstances. Klein believed that the healthy transition from the paranoid-schizoid experience to more whole-object depressive functioning had much to do with the constitutional balance of the life-and-death instincts and the external conditions of optimal mothering. The primary anxiety in this primitive position has to do with survival of the self rather than concern for the object.

On the other hand, the depressive position, a realm of psychological experience also discovered by Klein, is characterized more by the realization of dependent and hateful feelings towards the loved object, producing guilt and fear of loss. As opposed to earlier paranoid phantasies of ideal and loved objects versus other more persecutory and hated objects, now the subject faces the difficult reality of whole objects towards which one has a variety of feelings. This creates ambivalence, anxiety, and the desire to repair, restore, and rescue the injured other. Anxiety is still about the survival of the self if abandoned or punished by the offended and hurt object, but now the anxiety is much more about the well-being of the object. Obsessive and manic defenses come into play and projective identification phantasies are much more about the relationship to the object as opposed to the stark division of self and other found in the paranoid position.

Our more disturbed or difficult patients struggle with wanting a loving container and yet despising the idea that they need a container. The reasons for this volatile tension include the fury and sadness of never having one, the idea of only now finally finding one after a lifelong absence triggering pain, resentment, and sorrow, and finally, the loss and desperate envy that is evoked in seeing someone else able to provide a container because this must mean this other person already has access to their own soothing container. In the countertransference, the analyst may struggle to uphold the value of being a container as they repeatedly feel unused, unwanted, or aggressively prevented from being a helpful or healing container.

Instead, it is not uncommon for these more emotionally combative and turbulent patients to use the analyst as a vending machine to simply put in a coin, push a button, and get their expectations met on demand. If we don't conform to these demands and go along with this devaluing process, the patient becomes angry or feels completely misunderstood and abandoned. In these situations, there are often counter-transference feelings that evoke these very images of being used as a disposable container without any kind of enduring value, much like a spittoon, ashtray, or a toilet. After using us in this manner, some of these patients literally walk away. They have what they want and we feel completely devalued, destroyed, or defaced. Clinically, it is very important to understand exactly how and why these patients are finding their way into our minds and the details of why they want or need to use and misuse us in these specific ways (Joseph 1985, 1987, 1988, 1989; Segal 1987).

Case material

Grinberg (1990) has written an important article on how the analyst is led to fill a specific role in the patient's phantasy through what he calls projective counter-identification. An example of this emerged with one of my patients who explained how he grew up with a family in which "you felt close to everyone yet they never really talked to each other. We were never connected in any substantial emotional way." Gary left his small village when he was quite young to go to the big city and study. From there, he ended up leaving the country and going on to find success in college and in business. However, Gary remembers feeling quite alone and out of place, not fitting in with everyone in the big city and missing his little village and his family. But he tried to tell himself that "this was the way things go" and that he should just learn to deal with it as he felt he had no other choice.

Gary ended up very successful and independent, living far away from his homeland. As I said, from his description this path to career success was very lonely and stressful, especially when he was young and longed to be back with his family and friends. Gary tried to feel strong and independent, and to see himself as a wise grown-up, but the reality was that he felt like a little boy a long way from home. When I said this to him, Gary was able to take it in for a moment and I could see the pain and despair in his eyes. But he quickly retreated from that into his usual logical persona and told me, "We can't always have what we want in life and hardships make you tough in a good way. Being tough can help you along the difficult road of life."

Interestingly, my patient now has a job that takes him away traveling to distant countries two and sometimes three weeks a month. This means that we are unable to have a consistent connection, he is always away from his family, and he is unable to have any proper free time with himself. However, Gary rarely talks about his feelings about this. Instead, I am left to feel it and voice it. In passing, he may mention some frustrations, but then he quickly takes it back and says it's all just part of his job, part of how life goes, and so forth.

So, I am left being the one who feels left out, lonely, and longing for him to come back. In other words, through his use of projective identification, I think I have the feeling he described while growing up. In the counter-transference, I feel frustrated, left out, and justified to bring up this ongoing absence, as Gary seems to dismiss it without much thought or mention of our broken bond being a problem.

So, when Gary came back from a full month of being away and said nothing about it except to mention that he would be away for another week fairly soon, I felt frustrated and made a snide remark. I said, "I wonder how your family is coping with that?" In the transference I was clearly lashing out, hoping to make him feel guilty for neglecting his family, including his analytic family. Gary mostly ignored my comment. In passing, he said something about how they are used to it and they understand.

Later in the session, I offered him an extra visit in the weeks ahead to make up for the upcoming absence he had announced. In response, he said, "Oh. Why would I want to do that since we already have our usual appointment that week?" In a confrontive manner, I said, "Well, if this is going to work we need to meet more than we are. So, I'm talking about an extra visit." I felt I was doing all this in a pushy or upset way but again he was very neutral about it and agreed that one extra session was "okay." Of course, what was important to notice and interpret was that he himself would never ask for extras, as it might make him feel dependent, as if he actually missed meeting with me. Unfortunately, due to my counter-transference immersion that was quite overwhelming at that moment, I did not voice that; I only acted it out. As Grinberg (1962) has pointed out, I had been given a specific role in the projective counter-identification.

In the Modern Kleinian Therapy approach (Waska 2010a, 2011a, 2012), the analyst makes ongoing efforts to explore exactly how the patient seeks out the matching element, the matching object, or the matching role in the object to complement their own intra-psychic belief about self and other. So, if the patient feels they're a passive child who is used to being with an angry father, they will seek out those two matching elements in the transference relationship. It may be that they relate in the transference as the passive scared child or they may take on the role of the punitive and pushy father, molding the analyst into a bullied child role through the interpersonal dynamics of projective identification (Joseph 1997; Waska 2004, 2005, 2010c, 2010d).

Grinberg (1990) discusses how the patient is able to locate a facsimile of their phantasy objects in the analyst to begin that predicted encounter. Grinberg also notes that if they cannot locate it in us they will still try very hard to create it from scratch. I think this is a very valuable clinical insight and can be quite helpful in understanding the nature of the transference and its powerful influence on the counter-transference. Much of this has to do with the acting out, that can be very intense, and still quite subtle, which fuels the creation of the patient's unconscious expectations. These are the pressing and difficult moments in the counter-transference when the patient's phantasies are brought to life within the interpersonal aspects of projective identification. This all speaks to the vulnerability and fluidity of the counter-transference and the influential and seductive nature of transference. We must be on our toes at all times for the patient's internal efforts at communicating conflicts of love, hate, and knowledge through the phantasy directives of the life-and-death instincts and the potent vehicle of projective identification.

Case material

Sally is a patient whom I have met with only three times so far but she made her mark in my mind way before she even walked into my office. Sally was referred to me a year or two ago by another analyst whom she knew socially. Sally began calling me about every six to nine months wanting to make an appointment for me to treat her two grown children. Sally is sixty years old and her two grown children are thirty-five and thirty-seven years old. Each time I talked to her on the phone, I felt Sally was anxious, pushy, and emotionally forceful. I thought she was desperate to have me fix her two children but it was never really clear what she felt was wrong with them except that they weren't doing things the way she wanted and they were not being the kind of people that she thought they should be.

The way she related to me in the transference leading up to the actual appointment was an ordeal. Sally called to set up the appointment but she wanted her daughter to come in instead of her. Actually, she first insisted I meet with her son instead of her so that I could begin to fix him, but he told her he was definitely not coming in to see me. So, then Sally turned to her daughter and tried to convince her to come in. Finally, since neither child would come in, at my suggestion Sally reluctantly came in by herself. Once in my office, she immediately launched into stories of how both her children were in great need of psychological help. She outlined all the different ways in which they were unhappy and not accomplishing what they could or should have.

Sally told me that her son had struggled for years not being able to establish any significant career path but now had a job that "seemed okay." She went on to say that while he is finally more stable in his employment, emotionally he was angry, volatile, and prone to getting into fights with his sister and with Sally. Sally told me numerous stories of how her daughter and her son have disappointed her over the years by dating the wrong people, not going to church, and acting in ways that she didn't approve of. While Sally was intensely critical of her son and pushy in the transference for me to fix him and his problems, she was even more controlling, judgmental, and desperate about her daughter. According to Sally, her daughter was having even more problems than her son and was even more in need of my fixing.

In the counter-transference, I felt vindicated when Sally told me that her children frequently tell her she is critical of them and that is why they never want to get close or share anything about their lives with her. I thought to myself, "No joke! That is obvious from how Sally is!" As if she was responding to my critical thoughts, Sally said she knows she is critical and attributed that to "a long lineage in her family of nobody ever communicating with anybody about anything, especially feelings." She said she would like to be less critical but that's "just the way she is and she will never change. So that's that." Then, Sally quickly switched to telling me about all the problems her children have and how she wants to fix them.

On one hand, Sally does seem to feel very guilty and sad about having inflicted problems upon her children and admits that her critical nature has possibly left them the way they are. But, on the other hand, she quickly switches to not really seeing herself as a part of all these issues and instead just wants me to join in discussing these poor damaged creatures who desperately need fixing. So, I wondered if she was so overwhelmed with depressive guilt that she wanted to manically and magically repair these children and feel vindicated. Yet, I felt there was also something more sinister, primitive, or self-serving in her transference. It felt like an attack on the essence of who they were as people without any respect for their choices or admiration for their differences.

I noticed that in the counter-transference, as a result of her way of relating to me and to her children, I was starting to feel very critical of Sally. I felt as if she was nothing but a busybody sticking her nose into other people's business and trying to control them. I also felt that she had probably left her children with emotional scars and psychological problems because of her difficult nature and now she was just continuing that controlling judgment by offering them to me as damaged goods that need to be fixed.

At the same time, I did feel compassion for Sally as it seemed she was genuinely trying to redo something and make up for something she had done or imagined she had done. She wanted to somehow apply first aid to the destruction she imagined she had inflicted and wanted me to help her either ease her guilt or manically transform her children so as to never have to feel this pain and anxiety.

However, the majority of the transference was dominated by how Sally saw me as her instrument for controlling her children and her foot soldier who would make them into what she felt they should be. Sally wanted quick advice and immediate fixing. When I brought this up she insisted that she wasn't in therapy for herself and she would never come to see me for herself. She said she felt there was nothing much wrong with her and what was wrong could never be fixed. She was too old and change was impossible. Sally said she wanted her children to have a chance at living a better life and she wanted me to give her advice on how to fix them, what to do to make them turn around and be happy, sensible, and successful. Sally let me know that she was expecting that advice to come immediately, in the first session. When I pointed out her level of demand

and pressure, Sally said that she was getting frustrated because I had not yet given her any answers. In other words, rather than reflect upon my words and the meaning of her actions, she merely agreed with my observation as concrete fact. I was in fact letting her down by not delivering the goods fast enough.

In the second session, Sally once again let me know she was unhappy that I still hadn't given her the answers she wanted and therefore she wasn't sure if she would continue. She also threw in some other barbs and criticisms like "don't you have any better parking?" in which she devalued me for who I was and my failure to give her what she wanted when she wanted.

I noticed that Sally did seem to operate as a thick-skinned narcissist in that I could make fairly direct containing and confrontive observations of how she used her objects as well as more standard interpretations of why she related as she did without her reacting in any sort of overly sensitive or persecutory manner. Overall, Sally would take some of my comments in, but only for a brief moment and then discard them. When I began addressing her impatient transference with me and added that I realized there was probably some pain and anxious desperation underneath it, she quickly warned me that unless I gave her advice soon and unless she believed things were changing quickly with her children, she probably would not be coming any more. Sally said she didn't personally need anything from me. She told me that if her children came to me that would be great, but "otherwise it looks like this is going to be over soon."

Here, I commented that she seemed to have great difficulty needing me or having to depend on me for anything. I wondered if that left her feeling inferior and very vulnerable. Sally was able to take this in for a moment and it seemed to reduce her aggression and anxiety momentarily.

In meeting with Sally for the third session of her analytic treatment, the interaction with me in the transference seemed to be about the same. She focused intensely on her daughter, noting how very damaged and faulted her daughter was. Sally told me her daughter needed to see me and needed to be helped with all her problems. When I pointed out that she was seeing people as flawed and wrong and she was desperately trying to fix them and make them different, she basically agreed and literally said, "Yes. They are full of problems and they need to be fixed."

I asked Sally if it made her uncomfortable, now or in the past, to be more of a listener to others and to see what exactly their problems might be, to try to simply be there and understand instead of jumping in and controlling everything. She said, "I have always been a big failure at that and never known how to do that because no one did that in my family growing up." She added that "it was too late now." When I asked her about the details of this "too late now" despair, she again brought up her own family.

Sally told me how emotional closeness, forgiveness, and understanding were never available for her while growing up and that she "had to figure things out on the fly without having any guidance or direction." I interpreted that she now wanted to give her children guidance and direction, but with a vengeance. Sally said she simply wants to try to help prevent them from suffering ongoing disasters in their lives. Then, she started to focus on her daughter as being particularly problematic and how she was not doing well in life and failing at her career and in relationships.

In the counter-transference, I felt that Sally was extremely busy intruding into someone else's life, trying to control them, and that she was judging her daughter for being unhappy and for being a failure. In addition, I felt that she was intruding into me, controlling me, and judging me. I asked her if her daughter was really unhappy or was it that Sally was unhappy because her daughter never comes to her for help. Sally said it's just her "mother's sixth sense about her child" and that she thinks her daughter has been unhappy for a long time.

Sally said she wishes she could do something to help and then she reminded me how she expects me to provide answers on how to fix her daughter. So, I said that she had suddenly switched from momentarily exposing this more vulnerable desire to be a loving mother, to now pressuring me in the transference. She had risked telling me about her terrible feeling of not really knowing how to be a loving mother but then she switched to demanding that I do it for her in this "fix-it" way. She said, "Well, yes. It is too late to do anything else."

I asked her why it was too late to become more of a loving mother who listens and tries to understand her children's problems. I added that she seemed to have a hard time allowing me to be a loving mother to her. Sally said it's just too late for her and she's unable to do that. She said it's not about her anyway, it's about her kids. Then, she started crying and said she just wants to make sure that before she dies she knows that her daughter will stop being so unhappy. Again, in the counter-transference, my sense was that we did not know whether her daughter was unhappy or not. In other words, was this all a projection of Sally's unhappiness and desire for a good mother? I made that interpretation but Sally simply said she could tell her daughter was troubled.

So, based on the transference and counter-transference, as well as how Sally reacted to my interpretations, I began to think that this was more about my patient trying to heal herself via projective identification into her daughter, creating an experience with her daughter that she never had with her parents. But it was done in this very artificial, forceful, and fix-it manner.

Therefore, I interpreted that since Sally had not had a loving mother to go to for guidance and direction, she is now going to make sure that her daughter has that in any way that she can, whether her daughter likes it or not. She was forcing me to be the ideal mother who cares for her child, whether I wanted to or not. I said that this "with a vengeance" aspect of it seems to point to a great deal of grief and anger on Sally's part about what she did not have as a small child when she needed it the most. I said that there seems to be so much love, guilt, anger, and control all mixed together in the way that she's so quick to criticize her daughter. Sally was so fast to list all the different ways her daughter seems to be screwing up in her life, but Sally is also so impatient and desperate to get her help and fix her in all those departments.

In response, Sally said she feels that parents should have expectations for their children but her daughter feels those are just demands and criticisms. Sally said that they are only parental expectations. In the counter-transference, I agreed with her daughter.

During the course of this third session, Sally had also been talking about an event on the weekend that her daughter invited her to attend. Sally wasn't sure if she wanted to go. She felt a great deal of anxiety and uncertainty because her daughter had recently announced that she has a new boyfriend who is black and he would be there. Sally is very much against this new black boyfriend and "thinks it was an acting out and a very poor life choice on my daughter's part." Sally said it was an example of "her daughter screwing up again."

So, when I announced that the session was over and told Sally I would see her next week, Sally said impatiently,

> Wait a minute. This will only take a minute. This meeting with my daughter is happening over the weekend and I want to go but I feel very anxious about the whole thing. I don't like what she's done and I don't want to meet this black person. I wanted you to give me advice on what to do but you didn't. I'm here for help and I want to know what to do. So, I want you to tell me what to do! I need help.

I said, "I am glad to help you but we need time to do that. We are out of time today. Would you like me to set up a new appointment before the weekend so we have time to speak about this before the meeting with your daughter?" Sally said, "I just don't like how you end so abruptly and don't give me the time I need. You're not helping me. You're not giving me answers. I want to know should I go or not and you're not helping me!"

This was all said in an angry, impatient, and superior manner. I said, "I can help you but you need to make an appointment so I can help you. Do you want to make an appointment before next time?" Sally said, "No, I will wait for next time" and left. Again, I felt very pushed and manipulated, and somewhat threatened. I felt as if she had taken me by the collar and was demanding something from me. I felt I had to take a stand and let her know I would give something to her but she could not take it from me.

I think that in the transference, Sally was re-creating how she acts with her daughter. She was pushy and somewhat of a bully with me, wanting her way and wanting to get what she believed she was owed. I wanted to shut her down and draw limits, but, because I was being mindful of my counter-transference feelings, instead of reacting or slipping into an enactment, I responded in a way which also let her know I wanted to help her.

Overall, I think that Sally is so anxious about giving her daughter what she should have given her years ago but feels she failed at, she is now trying to force-feed her daughter with nourishment that she may not want or even need. In addition, I think Sally is so angry about not getting this loving, understanding container from her own parents that she is going to force it on to her children no matter what. During this process, she is manipulating me in the projective identification process to be the ideal mother she never had and feels she should have been to her children. In addition, she is putting her self-loathing into her daughter for me to transform.

I think Sally is desperate to create some kind of helping mothering situation which she did not have, and as a consequence this mothering desire is infused with envy, anger, revenge, and a lot of control. Thus, her mothering efforts come across as extremely predatory and pushy in the transference and apparently the same is the case with her daughter and son. In addition, she may feel so guilty about not ever bothering to listen to them or help them in an empathic manner that she is now aggressively trying to magically repair what she imagines to be broken, flawed, and damaged objects due to her corrupted mothering.

With the ending of the last session, I think Sally's chaotic control of the object was challenged in the transference and counter-transference. With my successful interaction with her, the therapeutic boundaries have been reset. We will probably have to enter that swampy morass again many times over.

Many disturbed and hard-to-reach patients are so disorganized internally and create such turbulence in the transference that you know sooner or later they are going to fade away or disappear without much discussion or notice. They are seemingly unmovable in this dedication to a primitive pathological organization (Steiner 1993) and its fixed belief system.

Overall, in the counter-transference with Sally, I feel Sally represents the "only a matter of time, this is going to end suddenly or sometime soon" type of difficult transference situation. This triggers a counter-transference retaliation feeling of "good riddance." This predictable but jarring exit may be abrupt but at the same time you feel it's been coming for a long time. This may happen after the patient has been in treatment for two or three years or two or three sessions. In other words, sometimes it is much more of a slow death and at other times it feels like a quick cutting of the throat; but, in either circumstance, we struggle in the counter-transference experience.

We must notice, understand, and resist the temptation to give up hope and simply retaliate. Instead, we must constantly struggle to regain our analytic balance and convey our hope, understanding, and fortitude, however small or tenuous, to the patient through interpretations and emotional containment.

Chapter 6

Patients marked by crippling loss

Counter-transference issues and early phase treatment

Ongoing scrutiny of our counter-transference experiences can not only reduce our tendency towards enactment but also help us understand our place in the patient's unconscious phantasy world. By examining our feelings, thoughts, and actions when immersed within the patient's transference efforts, we can gradually make sense of how the patient enlists us into their attempt to repeat and redo their core object relational conflicts (Ginberg 1990; Joseph 1985, 1989; Sandler 1976; Schafer 1997). We try to establish what role we are being asked to play and into what perspective we are being interpersonally and psychologically maneuvered. In alternating cycles, through the patient's reliance on projective identification, splitting, and manic undoing, we may be asked or forced to learn the part of the good object, the bad object, the lost object, or the idealized object (Spillius 1983, 1988). Or, we may be carried into an experience that parallels the patient's memorialized historical past, their desired future, or their current vision of self as colored by their particular and unique signature filter of the life-and-death instincts. Rescue and revenge, dread and desire, knowledge and denial, give and take, as well as sacrifice and entitlement are all part of countless internal tales of conflict and unconscious unrest that are played out in the transference and counter-transference. Three cases in which issues of loss were central illustrate the complexity of remaining focused and therapeutic when immersed within the counter-transference as a method to gradually understand, contain, and translate the unconscious efforts being made by the patient within the projective identification process (Feldman 1992, 1994, 2004, 2009).

Case material

Mary comes from a family where she says there is "absolutely no empathy, no listening, no understanding, and no talking about emotions." In its place, Mary says "there just was, and still is, a lot of criticism." Her mother would criticize her over and over again about everything and anything, telling Mary that she was failing to please her and falling short of her expectations. Probably as a result, my patient ended up approaching life in ways that indeed made it easy for her mother to criticize her. She was lazy at school, rebelled as a teenager, and between the ages of twenty and twenty-five was addicted to drugs, going to parties all the time, wasting money, and getting into trouble.

Mary is very angry and hurt to this day that her family, and her mother in particular, offered her no help or advice during that terrible period. Instead, they simply wrote her off as a troubled drug addict. Mary has come to me because she feels she is failing to be a good-enough wife and a good-enough mother. She sees many flaws in how she is managing her life. When she described various situations that she was unhappy with, it did sound as if there are reasons she should be concerned and ways she could improve. However, the way she thinks about herself and her life is very critical. Rather than learning and improving, Mary seems to just want to hunt down her flaws, label herself, and quickly sterilize those bad parts so that she can replace them with demanded and flawless replacement parts. Much like her description of her mother, Mary has very high expectations for herself to be perfect and to change from what she sees as her horrible imperfection to this new and improved self that she expects to find from her time with me.

So, I interpreted that Mary had enlisted me in this search for perfection and that she is running away from her own incriminations. Now, I have to help her find a way to quickly and immediately change into this good person. In the transference, there was intense impatience, desperation, and anxiety to reach this redeemed state and to reach it right away. Mary pressures me verbally, interpersonally, and facially to hurry up and deliver the goods. I interpret this quite often and she says she doesn't see the problem. Mary just thinks she should be "whipped into shape and that would be good."

Now, with this type of patient, the idea of the therapeutic container (Bion 1959, 1962; Cartwright 2010) is important because from Mary's own description she really had no parental container while growing up. Instead, she experienced a maternal vice in which she had to be perfect or she felt unwanted and bad. Now, in the transference, Mary was reacting negatively to me becoming her supportive, maternal container or understanding and interested analyst. She sees that as a silly distraction to the important work of instantly creating a new and perfect version of herself. In this way, I think she is trying to be omnipotent and independent as a way to rise above the incredible loss, anger, and humiliation of not having a mother upon whom she could count.

Recently, Mary told me about her husband being fired from his job. He had been anticipating this for a week and had been very depressed, but he never told Mary what the problem was. In trying to imagine why he was so down, she was worried that he was angry with her. She was very worried about it being all about her. So, when she found out that it was his own concern, she was momentarily empathic and tried to listen to him but very quickly told him to "get over it" and "hurry up and look for new job." She told him "to stop wallowing in pity."

In the counter-transference, I felt angry and shocked at her cruel treatment of her husband. I wanted to come to his aid. I made a few critical remarks to Mary about her lack of empathy before I noticed how I was treating her. Then, I was able to regain my therapeutic balance and realize I was probably, through projective identification-based transference influences, starting to step in and save Mary from her mother, as now played out by her as mother and husband as Mary.

From Mary's overall treatment of her husband and of herself, it was clear that she viewed her objects quite cruelly. On one hand, she seemed to genuinely want to help them and was concerned. But, at the same time, there was this savage verbal and emotional attack on herself and on her husband to improve, get over it, and move on.

I interpreted that she was applying the same sort of awful criticism that she felt from her mother to her husband, to herself, and to me. This seemed to be helpful. But her critical resistance to my interpretation, her avoidance of my non-critical way of thinking, and her reluctance to depend on me as an understanding container was pronounced. I interpreted that Mary was acting out her envy, grief, and sadness with me. With ongoing interpretive focus in this direction, Mary gradually seemed somewhat less anxious and less critical. This treatment process has only been in place for about four or five visits so we shall see how it proceeds from here. It will probably be rocky and tense for a while.

What I have noticed recently is that Mary is trying to instantly learn and change. So, what she earns is a false and grandiose progress. She came in last time and announced how much better she feels and how she has already learned so much.

In the counter-transference, I felt left out and cast as an audience member who should applaud her great and speedy accomplishments. I noticed how when I said, "You have only been here a handful of times. There is no way we have done that much yet," I was now being a critical audience member who was judging her performance as poor and not enough. So, here in the counter-transference, even accurate comments may be immersed within enactments of the patient's projective identification system (Joseph 1987, 1988; Mason 2011; Schafer 2002; Waska 2010, 2011a, 2012), creating projective counter-identification situations (Grinberg 1990) that are part of the patient's acting-out process of repeated internal demands and disappointments, or imagined fears and hoped-for victories.

So, we spent the rest of this session looking at how Mary was trying so hard to please me and please the demanding critic inside of herself. She had to prove that she was indeed getting better. I interpreted that, as with her behavior towards her husband, she was reluctant to allow me to be empathic or understanding and for us to simply take our time and see what she was feeling. Instead, we had to get it together and move on, not wallowing in pity as she put it. I told her she is enlisting me to be the one to convince her that it is okay to be loving, patient, and caring towards herself. Mary is reluctant to be vulnerable and depend on me or to forgive herself for being human instead of perfect.

In response, Mary said, "I know. But, it is hard. I am not used to it." So, we will continue our analytic journey to work through her experience of loss and her reactions to it as well as her resulting treatment of herself and all her objects. I will continue to monitor my counter-transference so that I can learn more about the role she asks me to play and how I may be acting out aspects of herself or her objects instead of containing and translating them. Perhaps, over time, Mary will "get used to it" and not feel so much dread and danger with change and learning (Waska 2005, 2006).

Case material

Lou was a man who intellectualized everything in his life. He avoided his feelings and tried to control everyone else's feelings as well. Everything and everyone was a potential problem that he could fix. In fact, he felt it was his duty to be the fixer, especially to those closer to him. Lou was reluctant to slow down and feel what was going on inside of him. He was very resistant to reflect upon himself in a psychological manner and looked outward instead. However, Lou was genuinely motivated to find a new way of relating with his family as he was "very disappointed in himself" when he saw himself acting angry or getting loud with his two young children and his wife. In this sense, his initial presentation was quite similar to how Mary started her analytic relationship with me.

In the first few months of treatment with Lou, I found myself feeling numb disinterest, listening to his mechanical rapid-fire verbal droning, relaying his countless efforts to "utilize" every aspect of my "advice" and "to implement the lessons of therapy." At the same time I felt quite a lot of compassion for Lou because he seemed to be so scared of facing a terrible feeling of loss, guilt, and a sense of being completely out of control. Some of these counter-transference ideas came from the affect in the room, the void of feeling between us, the way he used me in the transference, and his intense anxiety, but these feelings also came from knowing about Lou's history.

Lou was extremely close to his mother when growing up but then she died from an infection following routine surgery. Lou was literally at her bedside every day and held her hand as she drew her last breath. He was ten years old at the time and remembers "holding my mother in my arms as her last breath left her body." Lou told her that he would make sure to keep the family going, that everybody would remember her, and they "would always do their best to move on and ahead in life." At that point in his life, he tried to help the rest of the family to be happy and "move forward." Lou still has that as his main motivation in life.

I have pointed out that he was just a child, so he really had to convince himself he had the power to lead the family. I also noted how Lou took over his father's role, at least in his imagination. Lou told me how his father "really faded into the woodwork after mom died. He was there but really wasn't there."

Lou still feels that he is the captain of the remaining family members and works hard at "doing" instead of "getting bogged down in feeling." He is always focused on others to avoid being in touch with himself. Pushed by my counter-transference, I would tell Lou to slow down and stop trying to get me to fix him like he was trying to fix others. I interpreted that he was trying to control me now along with everyone else. He responded in a rather compliant way. As a result I felt that whatever I said next, Lou would take as his next set of instructions or assignment that, if carried out just right, would show him how to fix himself and others more efficiently. I told him this. I told Lou that he took my interpretations and quickly converted them into part of his phantasy of me giving him the nuts-and-bolts manual of how to live life better and fix others quicker.

I was aware that when Lou tried to do this in the transference, I felt pulled into catching him at it. At that point, I was immersed in the dynamic myself. I was suddenly trying to catch him and tell him how he should be doing it instead. The more he did it the more I did it until I was essentially telling him off. Now I was also trying to fix him and tell him the better way to be a good patient. By trying to monitor my counter-transference, I noticed myself acting out these dynamics with him. Once I regained my therapeutic balance, I tried to understand what exactly Lou was trying to do with me in his mind and the reasons he might be trying to position me or use me in this way.

During this particular session, Lou went on to talk about his family and his two young children whom he loves dearly. He felt very guilty about how he raised his voice when he's frustrated with them. Lou talked a great deal about how they seem to be developing well, how he treasures spending time with them, and how he wishes he had more time with them.

Then, he switched to talking about how he's happy to see them growing up in a very independent way. Lou emphasized how he's trying to teach them to be independent and do things on their own, just like how his father had taught him to be very mechanical and fix things. Lou said he's trying to pass this on to his children and let them grow up with a sense of "not needing to depend on anyone and that they can do everything for themselves."

The more Lou talked about this sense of independence and how he was trying to foster this individuality in his children so that they didn't need to depend on anyone, the more I started to feel as if he was imposing this independence upon his children and justifying it by saying it is simply good parenting. I had the sense he was pushing his kids away and forcing them to be independent, whether they liked it or not. I felt sorry for them and critical of Lou. The more I noticed my negative feelings towards Lou as a parent, the more I was able to realize that this was part of a counter-transference state that had been provoked in me by his projective identification efforts. I tried to use this information to formulate an interpretation.

So, I began to make some comments about how Lou grew up feeling as if he had no choice but to be very independent. He couldn't go to his mother any more after she died so he felt he had to be on his own, having to cope. I said that perhaps he was trying to pass that coping on to his children but that, in the process, he might be missing out on some chances to have a closer bond with them and savor the moments when they do depend on him. Lou wants to be close to them but, when he is, he feels anxious and worried about loss. In response to my comments, Lou seemed to start to become defensive and anxious.

One of the examples of independence Lou had been talking about was teaching his children to put on their own socks and shoes. When they say, "Daddy, please put my socks and shoes on" Lou says no, because "you know how to do it." Lou is proud of how they are able to take care of themselves that way.

I said,

> Perhaps to not face the pain of being dependent and close with your mother but then having to grow up so quick and so lonely, you try to cope by being super independent. But, maybe as a result, you end up creating some distance between you and other people, whether it here with me, in your family, or co-workers and friends.

I suggested that perhaps even though the children now know how to put on their socks and shoes, which is a good thing, Lou may miss out on selected moments where they simply want to be close to their father. They want him to put on their socks and shoes not because they can't or won't but because they want the chance to be with him in a special way.

Lou got even more defensive at this point. He asked me if I had children in an angry and accusatory manner. I asked him why he was asking and he said, "you have to have kids to know the facts about parenting. People with kids have the right to say things about kids but if you don't have kids you don't have that experience and you don't have that right."

In the counter-transference I felt suddenly on guard, anxious, and somewhat intimidated as Lou had sat up in his chair and stared at me with a look of challenge I had never seen in him before. I wondered if Lou could be violent. It was all quite startling but I managed to not react and simply keep my analytic standing. I asked Lou why at this moment was he challenging me and feeling so defensive. He slowed down and said he felt confused. I said perhaps it was because of what I said about the closeness that his children were asking for and his conflicts over independence versus dependence. In response, he stopped and looked shaken up.

After a moment of silence, Lou said he is really troubled by the idea that if his children are independent and can do everything for themselves they won't need him any longer, and, as they grow older and bigger, they will be growing apart and away from him. He said he will "lose them and be without them." He started crying. He said, "I feel like I will lose them if they grow up and take care of themselves. They won't need me anymore and I won't have them around anymore. I'll be all alone."

That was the end of the session but clearly Lou was now in touch with his core feelings of anxiety, depression, and loss. These very intense feelings also seemed to be a reliving of his terrible loss and separation from his mother when he was young and the self-imposed separation when he decided he must be independent and only take care of others.

Case material

I have seen John for approximately fifteen sessions so far. He is sixty years old and is very depressed. He suffers from a chronic heart condition which leaves him unable to do very much physically. John becomes exhausted after walking two or three blocks. He was diagnosed as a child with a chronic condition and told it would eventually become disabling when he was an adult. He was lucky to remain in good health up until a few years ago.

When growing up, John was extremely close to his mother who then died when he was five years old. John feels that this was the single most devastating event in his life and has defined all the events in his life going forward. Shortly after, his father got married again, to an angry woman who often physically abused John's sister and "left the household on pins and needles." John's father never stepped in. From examining the transference and counter-transference, John seems to repeat a dependent bond with me in which he searches for maternal warmth. He is quite passive, compliant, and eager to please, like a little boy who looks forward to our visits.

When he was a younger man, John was quite sociable and went to parties all the time and loved the night life. Now, he looks a little tired and sad. He seems lost in time, as he has a haircut popular with teenagers that doesn't quite fit in with a man of sixty years. John's tattoos were probably cool and modern twenty years ago but now look a little strange on him. He was married about twenty-five years ago but he ended up leaving his wife and subsequently divorcing her because she was into drugs and a fast-paced lifestyle. He wanted out of all that but in retrospect he feels that's "one of the biggest mistakes of my life."

The way he said "biggest of my life" was just like how he said his mother's death was the "single biggest event that shaped my life." Therefore, I wondered whether he felt he left his wife in the same devastating way as he felt devastated by his mother leaving him in death. With his wife, John feels he "could've maybe done something to change that relationship and make it a good one". So, the theme of giving up is important and has featured a great deal in the treatment and in the transference.

Years later, John met another woman and they had a child, who is twenty-five years old now. The way he describes the relationship with his daughter sounds somewhat immature, similar to how he seems with me. John says his daughter calls him daddy and behaves in ways that are common between a five or ten year old and their parent, not a twenty-five year old and her parent.

John told me he was fairly happy with his life until about five years ago when his heart condition suddenly became very severe. He had always felt lucky to have escaped the problem which his doctors predicted would start in his thirties, but now there was a very dramatic decline in his physical ability. Immediately, he had to start taking many medications and he feels exhausted all the time. This sudden shift in his life has brought out a very apathetic way of thinking and feeling in John which has arisen in the transference. While it is expected of him to be depressed over this major change in his life, this seems to be a much deeper and longer standing internal conflict that is suddenly taking shape externally.

In the transference, John conducts himself as someone at the end of the road with no more chances. He has given up. He has actually been on disability for the last two-and-a-half years and he has not worked at all. John doesn't even really think about working. He did try to get a job about five years ago and sent out many resumés, but it was at a time in the economy when no one was finding work so he virtually gave up after a year. In this last two-and-a-half-year period, John has not tried to get any work at all, reasoning that he is completely unemployable because of his age, health condition, lack of education, and lack of experience.

So, what I noticed in the counter-transference was how quickly I felt that John was either being lazy, faking it, or had lost all motivation and had collapsed into despair and depression. Indeed, he does talk about death as being something he looks forward to as a "wonderful thing that will be a reward for having been forced to go through this awful experience called life."

As a consequence of hearing this last part, I started to feel compassionate and sorry for him; but, mostly, I felt like a coach who steps in to say, "Wait a minute! You can still do it! There is a way that you can still do it." So, I feel both paranoid-schizoid (Klein 1946) and depressive (Klein 1935, 1940) responses and notice myself taking on the role of both self and object at different times (Sweet 2010).

When I notice that I feel I am drifting towards or being pulled towards this role of compassionate coach, I interpret to John that he seems to want me to brainstorm, hope, and give him guidance. In response, he agrees with me in a somewhat cute little boy way and says he looks forward to seeing me and always feels way better after he sees me.

A recent session is fairly typical of these dynamics. John came in and wanted to rearrange some of our appointments because he wanted to be with his daughter for an event. He said she would have to be all by herself at an all-day work event and "wanted some company so she didn't feel bored and lonely." I said that I didn't have any other appointments. He went back and forth about how he "needed to be there" for his daughter. I thought he was unable to see her as an independent adult and unable to feel confident enough to get what he wanted or needed with me instead of giving up and sacrificing it. I felt myself standing strong about our time together, thinking about how we must keep our appointment, how his daughter would survive, and how John deserved to stand up for himself.

I said all this and he agreed that it sounded somewhat trivial when he heard me saying it out loud. John said he could easily see me and could rearrange the time with his daughter. We discussed how he had been quick to see her as lonely and unable to cope, and therefore quick to give up on our appointment. Then, I had to take a stand for it on his behalf.

The next issue that came up was how John talked about being hardly able to afford to take a bus anywhere because he was so low on funds. He only has the money from disability for bus rides and often runs out before the end of the month. He has to borrow money from a relative to pay his rent. John uses food stamps for meals and government care to see me. John went on for a while about how down and out he was and I again brought up the idea that he seems to have given up on the idea of working and getting more money. He said he had thought a great deal about how I had brought up that idea at our last meeting and the link I made to his feeling of giving up on his first marriage. He said he had thought a great deal about my interpretation about how giving up seems to be an issue for him.

John said he feels he did give up in both circumstances but felt that the two incidents weren't really linked together because he wanted something better for his life when he left his wife but now he doesn't see anything better for himself in life. Indeed, John said he thought death would be a "welcome change." We went back and forth for a while about how he could work but then he would say, "I just can't work." I then pointed out that we were in that familiar debate where I am the one who was hopeful and championing him and he is the one giving up. John reflected on this for a while and then associated to a recent dream he had where he had been awarded an honorary position on a famous baseball team.

I pointed out, "After telling me how hopeless you are, you are now switching to a dream in which you are the new player of a very famous baseball team." He agreed, and said that in the dream he was very proud of getting the position and felt very excited. He told his friends about it and was very much looking forward to participating with the team. John showed up for the big game and in the locker room he noticed that his new uniform had been set out. When he went to put it on, the uniform fit just right but his special baseball shoes were way too big. I said it sounded as if he was excited and feeling confident but then worried about not being big enough to fit into this new, important role. He felt small and unable to take on the honor.

John said he had thought of something like that too. In the dream, he panicked that he could not play in the big game. He said he felt lost and hopeless but then it occurred to him that he knew the person who was in charge of baseball shoes and would go to him and request a proper size. So, he got up and went out of a door to find the shoe man but the door led out into a hallway to another door and then another hallway and another door. It became an endless maze through which John kept running. He was lost and not able to find the person. At this point in the dream, he almost gave up again but then the thought occurred to him that if he went back to the locker room he could probably use his own regular shoes and get away with it. He thought it wouldn't be optimal but that it might work. So then he started running back towards the locker room to use his own shoes and to successfully get out in time to play the big game. He tried frantically to get back to the locker room and was running and running, but in the end he could not find his way back.

At that point in the dream, John woke up in a panic. Then, with me, he spent a few minutes emphasizing how it didn't work out and how he failed to play with the famous team. I said that now he was feeling down and like a failure. John said it was true. He said it was all negative and it never worked out in the dream.

I pointed out how in the transference he was trying to convince me of how hopeless everything was. I pointed out that he was omitting or downplaying a big piece of the dream to me. In the very beginning, John was awarded the position on this famous team and on top of that he didn't give up in the dream. I told him he had the idea of finding the man with the right shoes and when that didn't happen he came up with his own idea of using his regular shoes. So, not only did John find himself with the great award of being asked to join the team but he tried to problem solve his way through some issues as well. Then, John said, "Well, it's only a dream and I'm on all these terrible drugs that make me have weird dreams anyway. So, it's all a drug-induced dream." He went on to say how most of the time he had nightmares anyway and this was just a strange anomaly in the sense that it was somewhat positive.

So, I then pointed out how dramatically he was taking up the gauntlet to prove to me what a failure he was and that this dream of success or near success was instead simply a fluke and drug induced. We talked about that for a while and then he associated to how good he feels coming to see me and how, no matter how down or depressed he feels, when he realizes he is due to come to see me he always feels better. John said he really looks forward to it and after he leaves from seeing me he always feels much better. I interpreted that now he was willing to feel more positive and feel better when it was in context of being with me, which was fine. But John seemed to have a very difficult time finding that same sense of pleasure, relief, and reassurance from himself as he did with me or as he did in the dream, where he was able to be an independent thinker, reliant upon his own talents.

John would rather have me be the constantly reassuring, soothing mother he could depend on, but to do so he had to feel hopeless and helpless.

Discussion

In the Kleinian approach, counter-transference has been a central factor in technique and in the understanding of how patients locate themselves in our mind and how they try to locate us into their mind. Bion (1959, 1962) has examined the idea of container and contained to better understand this process and how the interpersonal aspects of projective identification come alive and affect the counter-transference. Joseph (1989) has also noted how the patient draws the analyst into a variety of emotional experiences and how the counter-transference can illuminate the core elements operating in the transference. Grinberg (1990) and Segal (1981) have studied the clinical manifestations of intense and often violent projective identification and the resulting counter-transference acting out and insights that are both possible. Rosenfeld (1987) and Hinshelwood (1989, 1999) have discussed how the patient provokes, invites, begs, and demands the analyst to take on their projections and then they pay close attention to exactly how the analyst reacts or doesn't react to them. Thus, the transference is a projective one followed by a transference of reaction to what is perceived in the analyst in reaction to the patient's projective efforts. All this in combination makes for a complicated counter-transference experience but, if one can stay balanced and notice what is going on internally, it may provide vital interpretive information.

This chapter has presented three clinical reports in which counter-transference was an important factor in the treatment, and in the total transference (Joseph 1985) and complete counter-transference (Waska 2011b). In all three cases, the loss of a supportive, available, and soothing maternal object was a significant factor in the patient's pathological organization. Careful examination of the counter-transference helped to reduce enactment (Steiner 2000, 2006) and helped clarify the interpretive focus. In the patient's reliance on projective identification, there was an ongoing pull for the analyst to take on the role of helpful parent, accepting and guiding authority, and wise caretaker.

However, there was also a pull to become a critical and demanding object, impatient for change and relief. This in turn was reversed with the patient demanding immediate answers and special service as the analyst was left to feel judged and bullied. The analyst was supposed to just go along with the tone or emotional climate in the room without questioning it. This anger, demand, and assumption of perspective seems to be the result of losing the idealized object and trying to resurrect a stand-in copy, but ultimately finding a crude, controlling facsimile in the place of the hoped-for idealized object. This is because of the yearning for an ideal combined with the core fury, disappointment, envy, and grief projected into the hoped-for object and ultimately into the self.

All three cases are just beginning. However, careful here-and-now transference interpretations and ongoing considerations of the counter-transference helped keep the treatments focused on the patient's core object-relational conflicts and made it possible to begin establishing analytic contact (Waska 2007). This, in turn, creates an emotional template towards possible integration, change, and growth.

Part III

Modern Kleinian Therapy and the treatment of turbulent couples

Chapter 7

Modern Kleinian couples therapy

Pathological organizations and psychic retreats

This chapter offers a theoretical and technical view of how to understand, contain, and transform the couple's chaotic and destructive ways of relating and non-relating by tending to each party's individual phantasies and internal conflicts while also helping to work through the vicious cycle in which both parties often become enmeshed as a mutual method of repeating archaic wishes and fears. This mutual system of destructive, repetitive, and static projective identification is often crystalized into a highly resistive and resilient pathological organization (Rosenfeld 1987; Schafer 1994; Steiner 1990).

When this dysfunctional unconscious bargain breaks down, one or both parties often withdraw into individual psychic retreats (Schafer 2002; Steiner 1993) which leave them embedded in highly resistant emotional impasses. As a result, one or each party may need more individual focus before treatment can resume on the couple as a relational unit. Modern Kleinian Therapy is considered to be a helpful method with such hard-to-reach couples and an approach to gradually working through the intra-psychic and interpersonal elements involved.

Modern Kleinian Therapy

Modern Kleinian Therapy (Waska 2011a, 2011b, 2012, 2013) is a contemporary hybrid of classical Kleinian psychoanalytic technique and a clinical approach to working with more disturbed or complicated patients in either individual or couples treatment. Modern Kleinian Therapy uses a psychoanalytic focus to understand and work with both internal resistances and external roadblocks to psychological integration.

Clinically, we see many individuals and couples who tend to quickly subsume us and whatever we do or say into their pathological organization (Spillius 1988) with its familiar cast of internal characters. Modern Kleinian Therapy focuses on the interpretation of this particular transference process by investigating the unconscious phantasy conflicts at play and highlighting the more direct moment-to-moment transference usually mobilized by projective identification dynamics (Hinshelwood 2004; Joseph 1988, 1989; Segal 1997). Bion's (1962) ideas regarding the interpersonal aspects of projective identification, the idea of projective identification as the foundation of most transference states (Waska 2004, 2010a, 2010b, 2010c), and the concept of projective identification as the first line of defense against psychic loss (Waska 2002, 2010d), difference, or separation all form the theoretical base of this clinical approach.

Therapeutically, we strive to move the couple into a new experience of clarity, vulnerability, reflection, independence, change, and choice. Clinically, we support this psychic change (Feldman 2004) by attempting to foster and fuel an ongoing level of analytic contact with the couple and with each party of the couple, creating a potential psychological moment of new, unrestricted, uncensored thinking and the opportunity to approach the self and the other in new, more creative ways. As such, analytic contact (Waska 2007) is defined as the sustained periods of mutual existence between self and object not excessively colored by destructive aggression or destructive defense.

These are moments between couple and analyst as well as between both partners of the couple when the elements of love, hate, and knowledge as well as the life-and-death instincts are in sufficient balance as to not fuel, enhance, or validate the patient's internal conflicts and phantasies in those very realms. These are new moments of contact between self and other, either in the mind of the patient or in the actual interpersonal realm between patient and analyst. These are found fragments of peaceful and pleasurable attachment that provide proof and hope that need, change, and difference can be beneficial and worth risking. Internal dynamics surrounding giving, taking, and learning as well as the parallel phantasies of being given to, having to relinquish, and being known are all elements that are usually severely out of psychic balance with these more challenging patients. Analytic contact is the moment in which analyst and patient or both parties of the couple achieve some degree of peace, stability, or integration in these areas or at least allow for the possibility of calm, change, and learning.

So, analytic contact is the term for our constant quest or invitation to the couple and individually for the found, allowed, and cultivated experiences that are new or less contaminated by the fossils of past internal drama, danger, and desire. These moments, in turn, provide for a chance of more lasting change, life, and difference or at least the consideration that these elements are possible and not poison. Paranoid (Klein 1946) and depressive (Klein 1935,1940) anxieties tend to be stirred up as the couple's safe and controlled psychic equilibrium (Spillius and Feldman 1989) come into question. Acting out, abrupt termination, intense resistance, and excessive reliance on projective identification are common and create easy blind spots and patterns of enactment for the analyst (Feldman 1994; Grotstein 1994). When this situation continues unchecked, it is common for one or both members of the couple to flee to their own private psychic retreat.

Pathological organizations, psychic retreats, and couples treatment

Pathological organizations are rigid and complex systems of defense that couples use to avoid unbearable persecutory and depressive anxieties and to distance themselves from the internal and external reality of self and other. With pathological organizations, both parties exist within a projective identification system that provides a controlled and rationed degree of genuine connection allowing for intense control over fears of the unknown. This results in a volatile yet stable mix of gratification and conflict without many moments of peace or contentment. It feels safe and familiar, matched to archaic, internal conflicts regarding love, hate, and learning. Therefore, limiting and confining patterns of pathological repetition bind the couple together in a known but suffocating web.

These emotionally locked and emotionally starved couples demonstrate highly destructive narcissistic cycles in which certain parts of the self act against other parts of their partner, resulting in a variety of sadomasochistic, perverse, or addictive relational profiles. These couples desperately attempt to create a fragile and precarious mutual avoidance of both paranoid and depressive fears, but in the process eliminate any hopeful object-relational balance that comes from the normal experiences of both positions. Pathological organizations are destructive states of psychic equilibrium, providing a temporary sense of control and respite but ultimately removing the couple from the healing aspects of relational reality and the working through of both paranoid and depressive issues.

If the couple's pathological organization starts to be more overwhelming than secure due to excessive projective identification cycles creating increasing paranoid or depressive anxieties, one or both parties will seek escape and defense. If the destructive unconscious relational bargains (Waska 2005) that make up their bond seem to be collapsing or if one party feels the other party has ceased to play their role in that familiar bargain, one or both parties will withdraw into their own private psychic retreat.

With psychic retreats, the individual will seek a protective shell, haven, or refuge from overwhelming phantasies of loss, annihilation, persecution, and guilt which they experience in the relational bond. In treatment, we observe these patients embedded within their internal fortress and out of reach. They feel safely out of touch with reality and their threatening or threatened objects, but also out of touch with the understanding and help of their partner and their analyst.

The pathological organization is an unhealthy system of paranoid and depressive functioning in which excess projective identification links the two parties into an eternal playing out of archaic trauma and imagined wishes and entitlements. Both parties are able to tolerate the mutual perversion of paranoid and depressive relating to form an unhealthy but functional relational system. When the paranoid or depressive phantasies and conflicts of the pathological organization become overwhelming, the system breaks down and one or both parties flee to their psychic retreats. Steiner (1987, 1992) has described the psychic retreat as an inner limbo in which the patient hangs between the worst elements of the paranoid schizoid position and the depressive position.

The most common way we see a couple's pathological organization break down is when the couple's relationship becomes dominated by paranoid-schizoid anxiety and the associated defenses of splitting, idealization, devaluation, as well as the acting out of the death instinct, in which they seek to kill off any difference, need, growth, or change.

What we observe clinically with couples rooted within the paranoid-schizoid position is an immature, primitive state of mind, in which objects and the self are experienced in one-dimensional, black-and-white chunks carved out by primitive splitting and excessive projective identifications. In fact, this state of mind is dominated by projective identification and splitting, and leaves the subject feeling persecuted and abandoned by bad objects or united with and loved by idealized objects (Joseph 1987; Segal and Britton 1981; Steiner 1989).

Klein believed that the healthy transition from the paranoid-schizoid experience to more whole-object depressive functioning had much to do with the constitutional balance of the life-and-death instincts and the external conditions of optimal mothering. The emotional struggle of the life-and-death instincts we all go through in life are intensified in the couple's constant negotiation of need, dependence, separation, and difference. The results of this relational struggle are shaded by the manner in which each party becomes an adequate parental container for the other or an inadequate, fragile, or rejecting container/parent.

This is often very evident in couples where their core of particular crisis points has to do with states of need and how the needy partner reacts to their dependent feelings as well as how their partner responds to their show of need. Of course, issues of control, rejection, entitlement, shame, denial, and resentment all arise in this arena. If the couple's primary mode of operating in their pathological organization is more paranoid, issues of need and desire will be felt much more dramatically because the primary anxiety in this position has to do with survival of the self rather than concern for the object.

On the other hand, the couple's reactions of need, difference, or openness will be different if their pathological organization is dominated by more depressive position anxieties. This is a psychological realm characterized by the realization of dependent and hateful feelings towards the loved object, producing guilt and fear of loss. As opposed to paranoid phantasies of ideal and loved objects versus other, more persecutory and hated objects, now the subject faces the difficult reality of whole objects towards which one has a variety of feelings. This creates ambivalence, anxiety, and the desire to repair, restore, and rescue the injured other. Anxiety is still about the survival of the self if abandoned or punished by the offended and hurt object, but now the anxiety is much more about the wellbeing of the object. Obsessive and manic defenses come into play and projective identification phantasies are much more about the relationship to the object as opposed to the stark division of self and other found in the paranoid position.

Most couples we work with are not yet able to access or participate in these more mature developmental stages. However, the pre-depressive states of persecutory guilt and annihilation anxiety are often encountered. It is common to see couples come in for help because their psychic equilibrium within the pathological organization has been disrupted by these types of anxieties. This leads to one or both parties becoming embedded in their private psychic retreats, creating a severe imbalance or near collapse of the relationship. We struggle in the countertransference because we hope to help the couple find a more mature and mutually healthy way of living while the couple often unconsciously only wants help in returning to their pathological organization before terminating treatment.

When one party withdraws into a psychic retreat, they experience a temporary escape at the cost of mental impairment. Steiner (1993) considers such withdrawal to be understood simultaneously as an expression of destructiveness and a defense against it, serving a temporarily protected space but at the price of impaired contact with reality.

The psychic retreat is experienced by the patient as a safe haven and refuge from the unbearable persecutory and depressive anxieties of the pathological organization. What the patient does not like about himself or about his part in the couple's problems is expelled by means of projective identification, leading to a vicious cycle of having to hide or withdraw from the oppressing elements of the other and the couple's relationship (Feldman 1992; Joseph 1987; Rosenfeld 1983). Steiner (1993) has noted how psychic retreats effectively block the reversal of projective identification. They prevent the painful mourning associated with regret, separation, and the ongoing evolution necessary in healthy couple relating.

Psychic retreats prevent change, mourning, and growth but they also involve sadomasochism. There is a sadistic pleasure in refusing and frustrating the analyst's wish to be helpful or the other partner's efforts at healing. In addition, there is masochistic pleasure in depriving oneself of the possibility of improving, creating a mutual sense of never finding any hope of a better life. Here, the workings of the death instinct in psychic retreats and pathological organizations are evident.

Psychic retreats create a moment frozen in time where growth is avoided and pain is never forgotten. When the pathological organization is breaking down, both parties often feel trapped in the near-psychotic anxieties of the paranoid-schizoid position or the pre-depressive position fears of annihilation and eternal loss so that they flee to the emotionally frozen sanctuary of the psychic retreat. Only when they feel more in control of the object will they return to the familiar psychic equilibrium of the pathological organization.

The concept of pathological organization refers to the combination of narcissistic perverse, addictive, and sadomasochistic elements that infect the couple's relationship but also serve to provide a dubious psychic equilibrium. The internal dread that binds many couples together creates a mutual reliance on excessive projective identification processes to avoid and escape various phantasies and anxieties, resulting in the establishment of a pathological organization that both parties believe provides them with security and sustenance. Separation, loss, difference, and individuation are unwanted, intolerable, and villainized in the pathological organization.

Without the excessive projective identification cycles that make up the pathological organization, these couples would not find any mutual gratification and a sense of finding the missing pieces of themselves. But this sense of wholeness by being with their partner is in parallel to the matched repetition of numerous archaic conflicts and object-relational impasses that provide familiarity and control but stagnation and corruption of the mind.

In a sense, this description fits many couples who live much happier lives in a healthy harmony with each other. The couples examined in this chapter exist in such cycles but with a far greater and graver intensity, creating a much more ominous and perpetually painful relational bond.

As a result, pathological organizations provide couples with a precarious psychic equilibrium by dismantling the more alive and porous bond that allows change, reality, and growth. Normal fluctuations and a healthy balance between paranoid-schizoid phantasies and depressive conflicts are avoided as the potential vibrancy of the relationship is put on hold in exchange for predictable, controlled repetition of ancient desires, unresolved battles, primitive fears, and intense entitlements. As a result, pathological organizations in couples are highly resistant to change and pose considerable technical challenges in analysis.

Couples treatment

Sandler (1976) has described the unconscious roles patients assume for themselves and others and the interpersonal and intra-psychic means they take to actualize those roles. Sandler describes the induced counter-transference created by the patient's relationship to an object that is both repeated and defended through the induced role relationship with the analyst.

In understanding the unconscious processes that take place in the therapeutic setting with couples, from a more Kleinian perspective one may also consider the more subtle processes in which aspects of either party's mind are defensively expelled into each other or into the analyst. The Modern Kleinian Therapy approach helps the analyst recognize the precise ways in which the couple's intolerance for their joint or individual mind and the conflicts within it drive the creation and maintenance of the pathological organization, which with its intense projective identification cycles manipulate, alter, or corrupt the analyst's capacity to think or feel (Hinshelwood 1999).

In examining, the internal, interactional, and interpersonal roles couples are loyal to, we notice that these are not just simply roles that signify a type of person with certain attributes but an entire way of relating, thinking, acting, and feeling. One or more aspects of thinking or not thinking become highlighted through projective identification and enabled in the counter-transference. One or both parties of the couple show us how locked in they are to certain loyalties or certain dread regarding love, hate, and knowledge as these phantasies unfold within the unconscious object-relational phantasies that become apparent in the analytic setting.

This creates the intense and often surprising restrictiveness of the transference and the resulting rigid counter-transference experience. Thinking of the complexity of this role assignment process, the adding or subtracting of unconscious phantasy and inner conflict to the actual external couple relationship, as if there were no difference between internal and external or reality and phantasy, has a far-reaching impact on the clinical situation.

One is impressed with how affected we are as a result by the total transference situation (Joseph 1985). Therefore, when working with couples so loyal to pathological organizations and so embedded in their psychic retreats, we must also manage and utilize the complete counter-transference (Waska 2011a, 2011b, 2012).

The clinical and theoretical stance of both classical and contemporary Kleinians with regard to the concept of projective identification and the life-and-death instincts is helpful in finding a clinical foothold when conducting couples therapy. This is especially true with fragile, primitive, and turbulent patients prone to paranoid-schizoid (Klein 1946) anxieties. Analytic observations (Waska 2012), containment (Cartwright 2010), and interpretive translation of the complex conflicts within the couple and within each party are vital technical tools in fostering the possibility for successful analytic contact and gradual resolution of complicated object-relational phantasies regarding the danger of change (Waska 2006). This is a phantasy of danger in each party and often a mutually shared couple's fear of change that fortifies and verifies the pathological organization and their loyalty to it.

As a result, the more disturbed borderline and narcissistic couples we often encounter require a great deal of therapeutic flexibility rooted in traditional psychoanalytic technique but honoring the additional complexity and chaos inherent in couples work. The analyst must alternate their focus on each party's phantasy of destructive, persecutory, or reactionary conflicts before ever being able to address the mental dynamics of the pathological organization they have mutually established. When both parties are developmentally unable to take in and tolerate the idea of a "we" or "us," or the more mature acceptance of a self-contribution or responsibility for the condition of the relationship, the analyst must first work with the primitive experiences and phantasies of masochism, injustice, persecution, entitlement, and action that occur in their private psychic retreats and the crudely assembled but fiercely defended pathological organization.

These are the internal aspects of psychic chaos that occur as a result of conflicts between life-and-death instincts, in particular as defined by Hanna Segal (1993). The life-and-death instincts, combined with excessive projective identification mechanisms, form the base of the pathological organization as a dysfunctional solution to intense internal conflict and cause the breakdown of the false but familiar security of the pathological organization. This leads to one or both parties fleeing to shelter in a psychic retreat.

Modern Kleinian Therapy considers this distinct anti-life, anti-growth, or anit-change force to have an upper hand in some patients. The death instinct seems to arise most violently in situations of need, envy, difference, separation, or the risk of growth and change. In the form of an aggressive defense, the death instinct is behind the enduring pathological organizations and destructive yet enduring and gratifying forms of psychic equilibrium found in our more challenging couples.

Hanna Segal has defined the death instinct as the individual's reactions to needs. Either one can seek satisfaction for the needs and accept and deal with the frustrations and problems that come with those efforts. This is life-affirming action or the actions of the life instinct. This is life-promoting and object-seeking. Eventually, this leads from concerns about the survival of the self to concerns about the well-being of the other.

The other reaction to needs is the drive to annihilate the self that has needs and to annihilate others and things that represent those needs such as the very bond of the couple's relationship. Kleinians see early external experiences of deprivation and trauma playing as important a role as internal, constitutional factors in the ultimate balance between the life-and-death forces. These early phantasies and experiences of trauma are repeated in the couple's pathological organization and seem to provide a form of painful glue that keeps the couple together but also prevents them from changing or acquiring new ways of seeing each other and therefore themselves. Each party's reaction to need in themselves and in their partners is a critical area of focus in the Modern Kleinian Therapy approach to couples treatment.

Whenever possible, interpretation of the mutual projective identification-based transference state that creates a pathological organization is critical and those interpretations would include these conflicts between life-and-death instincts that either intensify the pathological organization or cause one or both parties to pull away into their only psychic retreats. Initially, and often for a very long time in the treatment, the interpretations have to be centered on each party's own psychic retreat and its defensive structure and the unconscious phantasies regarding self and other that drive it.

In other words, the reality of most couples treatments involves spending long periods of time on either one or the other party and then often switching to the other party's barricaded retreat before being able to explore the pathological patterns which both usually share. The analyst is limited by the two psychic retreats to interpreting the separate components of the projective identification unit as opposed to the relational pattern and system. In other words, the individual psychic retreats that emerge in couples treatment must be dealt with alongside the pathological organization the couple has solidified over time. The transference to the analyst usually emerges in stronger detail when interpretations regarding defense or change are made, endangering the psychic equilibrium of the couple's pathological organization or challenging the embedded psychic retreats.

The task of analysis is to work on these aspects of the couple. As a result, the couple can slowly elect to build a new and healthy psychological shelter that they both feel safe in together. When they wish, they can emerge individually or as a couple to face the world internally and externally in a different manner, no longer victim to archaic projective identification processes but now simply traveling to and from their emotional "home base" and enriching both places in an ongoing positive feedback loop.

In order to assist these more fragmented and skittish couples towards this potential psychic shift, the analyst must be constantly willing and able to move from moments of individual therapy with one or the other party to moments of engagement with the pathological organization to which both parties are loyal, and then back to assisting one or both parties with the difficulties of emerging from their retreats. Potentially, the analyst can assist both parties in creating this new mutual membrane, a new healthy shelter that now provides a growth-enhancing projective identification match and an island of gratification away from the day-to-day conflicts of the real world. Long-term, committed relationships have this respite and mutual support quality without the stagnant repetition of trauma so common in pathological organizations.

One form of resistance or acting out encountered with couples whom we see is the turning away from truly knowing each other in a new complementary way because it involves the depressive position realization of various truths about the nature of self and object. The fallibility, the availability, the limits of devotion, and the vast complexity of the object are all part of what most couples resist knowing. In the splitting of primitive unconscious object-relational dynamics, each party is hateful of the bad internal objects they feel they do know but cannot control as well as declaring pathological loyalty to the pleasure they experience with the idealized archaic objects of which they feel in complete control. But, to truly know their partner means that they have to give up and lose these former and familiar phantasy objects in exchange for the actual person they are now with.

Issues of knowing, loving, and hating are always areas of conflict (Feldman 2009; Hargreaves and Varchenker 2004; Segal 1981) but are particularly complicated with the difficult couples we see, usually within the borderline or narcissistic realm. These are individuals who cannot or do not want to face the exposure to reality that comes with emerging from their individual psychic retreats and giving up the psychic equilibrium of their mutual pathological organizations. Realizing you don't completely control or know your partner of many years is both very frightening but also an exciting learning opportunity. This state of mind is often discovered towards the end of a successful couple's treatment.

Case material

I have seen A and B in analytic couples treatment twice a week for four years. Initially, their relationship was emotionally abusive, volatile, and sometimes violent. They had little ability to manage their impulses. Communication was almost non-existent. A and B simply reacted to each other and used each other as projective puppets. Their pathological organization was very destructive and often became so chaotic that they both spent much of their time relegated to their psychic retreats, lobbing insults and ultimatums from their emotional bunkers. Much has changed and improved over the four years of treatment. However, there are many layers and degrees of conflict we still struggle with.

With some couples, much of the work is with each party's individual psychic retreat, its signature projective identification profile, and associated defenses. Other couples require the analyst to grapple with the mutually established pathological organization and its rigid themes of destructive relating and non-relating as well as the perverse system of gratification which neither party typically wants to relinquish.

For A and B, there has been an ongoing fluctuation from pathological organization to psychic retreat. When the psychic equilibrium of the pathological organization began to break down, each party entrenched themselves back into their psychic retreat. Then, gradually, A and B would feel safe and more in control, electing to re-establish the pathological organization in which there were genuine aspects of caring and love and a precarious ability to function together. They were able to give balance to each other in ways that were psychologically significant but that semi-healthy equilibrium quickly shifts to a poisonous blend of mismatched conflict. For A and B, even the more stable aspects of their pathological organization easily drift into patterns of sadomasochistic relating, bringing to life the destructive pattern that leaves them emotionally stagnant, broken, and hopeless.

This return to nothingness and emotional warfare is part of how the pathological organization is shaped by the death instinct. Life, change, need, and gaining new insight into self and other are all warded off by killing the opportunity for closeness, clarity, negotiation, acceptance, and the giving up of what one wants in self and other for what really is and what potential really is possible between self and other.

An example of the pathological organization A and B frequently assembled for themselves and with which they engaged me in the transference was a highly charged mother/child dynamic. A would tell her husband what to do in a very demeaning manner and be critical both in tone and message. She acted like a very controlling, hostile, and never satisfied mother who scolds and orders her child around. B would be silent and obey these orders but would later explode in rage, leaving A devastated and feeling abused once again. Or, B would react like a rebellious child, not doing his homework and behaving irresponsibly. In the past, this included him having secret fun behind her back which has included drinking, drugs, and affairs. This would provide A with the weapon of righteous rage, masochism, and revenge which seemed very important to her overall way of experiencing the world but obviously left her in constant despair and anxiety.

So, often in the sessions, I was interpreting the mutual state of back-and-forth judgment, attack, and resentment. Even over time, as they grew and changed, this continued. Now that B was able to contain his anger, he could admit to and apologize for his temper and selfish ways. However, when he asked A to consider her side in whatever dispute was happening, she was unable to participate in this move towards a more depressive position of healthy mutuality. Instead, she felt it was "unfair, an attack of blaming, evidence that he was lying and not being accountable" and she reverted to feeling "devastated about all the horrible abuse over the years." This last part was not an angry grieving triggered by forgiveness or acceptance, but a use of the past as a weapon to avoid the current challenge to her psychic retreat. At that point, I had to shift to a focus on her individual conflicts and defensive stance. So, in a projective identification-based transference moment, now A did get the focus to be all about her instead of the threatening mutuality and potential growth that B had initiated or invited her to join him in.

An example of the normal pathological organization that kept A and B together but left them feeling empty and discontented occurred fairly recently. A was out of town on a business trip. B was going to meet some friends for dinner. A called him and said she needed his help in deciding what to do regarding a project she was handling. For years, A has been working at a job that vastly underpays her and that B feels is a great waste of time, energy, and money.

Since A misses 10 to 20 percent of our sessions, I have pointed out that she is also putting the job over our sessions as she can choose whether or not to travel. I have also pointed out that A never speaks about how the travel leaves them both alone and separate for no apparent good reason, but A insists that the frequent travel is important to her because it is a business her father owns and she wants to be helpful in any way she can. B has pointed out that her father does not really need her help. B feels A is often choosing to side with her father and the dead-end job than to be with him. So they often fight about it. Yet, she still asks for his advice and he still gives it to her, and then they fight about the details.

This is exactly what happened again. B ended up in his car on the phone with her, giving her advice while his friends started dinner without him. He told me he wanted to help her and when she told him what she was going to do he told her it was a very bad idea and recommended that she do almost the opposite. A agreed and thanked him, and B went off to dinner. The next morning they were talking and A told B that she had gone ahead and made the choice B was so against. In the session, B told me,

> I lost it. I blew up. I couldn't believe I had put all that work into it for her and then she didn't do what I said. I started yelling at her, cursed, and hung

up. Later, I called to apologize but she has not returned my call for days now. But, I still feel furious that she ignored my suggestions.

So, I now had to address two areas in the couple. There was the pathological organization and there were their individual psychic retreats, and both were suddenly in play. When A returned from her trip, I interpreted that they had slid right into a very familiar pattern that they are both loyal to, but they also end up very angry and hurt from this conflict into which they settle so readily. A asks B to be a part of something he thinks is wrong to begin with but he doesn't voice his opinion out of fear of conflict, so he feels controlled. A becomes anxious obsessive, and controlling about the job problem, and draws B into that endless cycle of what to do, but she demands he only give her something she agrees with. B then says what he really thinks and A ignores it. B is outraged and lashes out; A feels abused and lashes back. They fight and A sees the fight as evidence that B is as bad as ever and goes into hiding, refusing to talk, refusing to accept his apology, and refusing to look at her part in the problem.

Usually, this makes B even more angry and helpless, causing him to lash out some more. However, he has been able to avoid this over the past six months, creating a marked difference in his participation in the pathological organization. As a result, they have been operating in a healthier manner for some of the time. But, overall, A has withdrawn more into her psychic retreat out of fear and anger about this shift in their psychic equilibrium. I interpret that they both pull me into the pathological organization and react in predictable ways to ignore, pervert, or fight my observations.

So, as illustrated above, the chance to work with them on their pathological organization system is usually short lived and choppy. It is a matter of time before one or both withdraw into their psychic retreats. For B, this means that he retreats to a paranoid-schizoid mode of being in which he wants immediate recognition for what he says or gives, and lashes out if he feels forgotten or used. He becomes ultra-sensitive to this phantasy of neglect.

Thus, in the couple's session just reported, I turned my attention to working with B to understand, contain, and translate how he put himself in a position to feel used or ignored and why it was so crucial for him to be right and for his opinion to be the one and only that A chose. Only when we could find some clarity to this internal conflict could we look at why he was not able to see how A was in fact using him or controlling him in reality and why he did not speak out to that and protect himself in some way. Of course, now I still had to help A to consider her aggressive anxiety over having to know the answer to her work problem and to solve it immediately, no matter what. She wasn't really asking for advice, she was searching for the best weapon to do battle with her imagined foe at work and to not feel as if she lost in this battle to know the perfect answer.

At this point in the couple's analytic treatment, A and B still rely on their pathological organization much of the time. However, they have allowed themselves to mutually move rather more into the realm of depressive functioning and its associated rewards of whole-object relating. These periods of new clarity, trust, commitment, and acceptance are not stable or lasting, but this new healthy "ask and offer" has begun to replace the more drastic and hurtful "give and take" of before.

Discussion

The reason why deep and lasting couples work from a psychoanalytic perspective is so complicated and difficult is that the analyst is working with two separate psychic retreats as well as a unified pathological organization. This is a rigid psychic equilibrium that yearns for change yet dreads and resists change. In others words, the status quo is vital even if defeating and constricting. If the phantasy is that a partner is being unfair or mean, the pathological solution is to punish them, force them to be fair by being even more selfish than they are, or to match detachment with even more severe distancing. The pathological organization in couples is maintained by this constant striving for pathological solutions to fears, wishes, and internal demands. In addition, the individual psychic retreats are maintained as escape hatches and fortresses of sealed-off aggression and defensive retaliation in this ongoing stand-off.

The analyst is often seen as asking one or both parties to give in or give up their methods of control and security, which is experienced as frightening, shaming, and unbearable. Therefore, work must be done at the level of each party's unconscious phantasy state and existing object-relational conflict perspective regarding self and other. Interpretations need to be aimed at this level of fear, narcissistic challenge, and control in order to be helpful and effective. The complicated therapeutic journey with couples involves this slow emergence from individual psychic retreats, a return to static chaos of the pathological organization, and a gradual transition to a new and healthy system of mutually beneficial projective identification in which need, difference, and separation are honored.

Chapter 8

Couples treatment from a Kleinian perspective

Kernberg (2011) has described the more immature or paranoid-schizoid (Klein 1946) couples who are limited in their capacity to love each other fully. They operate in more of a transactional relationship or barter system based on feelings of unfairness, lack of trust, and narcissistic reaction. There is a lack of genuine tolerance, forgiveness, gratitude, curiosity, and learning. A mature dependency that allows for joint goals with respect for differences is missing, with crude power struggles in its place. Limit setting and boundary formation are vital between partners, and between couples and the analyst; but in couples with severe relational problems, limits and boundaries are often casualties of the splitting (Siegel 1998) that contributes to their mutual problematic pathological organization (Steiner 1993). The excessive reliance on projective identification so commonly at the core of the couple's pathological organization results in relationships that are either without any sufficient relational and emotional boundaries and mutually established limits or they are suffocated by rigid and demanding rules and persecutory assumptions that dictate and constrict the relationship (Segal 1997; Spillius 1988).

Healthy relationships are marked by negotiable need, reasonable desire, manageable disappointment and loss, and acceptance with forgiveness. Evolution of need is followed by gratification and gratitude with further negotiation and change that allows for more loss and gain within a balance of frustration and joy for what one cannot have, what one does have, and what one can strive towards having. In addition, the idea of "having" is experienced as both a private, selfish, "me" reward as well as the warmth of what one can obtain as part of a team, a pair, a partnership, and a unity of two separate parties operating as one.

These are all elements that are severely missing or askew in the couples we usually see in treatment and are therefore elements we try to help couples realign to or to discover for the first time. Dicks (1967) has noted how partners are often chosen for attributes that complement aspects of each other's internal world, allowing for a ready-made projective identification match and repetition of familiarity, unresolved conflicts, and relational dynamics. This creates healthy projective identification-based relationships for some and for others leads to a rigid pathological organization system that allows for primitive gratification and security but limits true intimacy, growth, need, and difference (Joseph 1987).

Unresolved family-of-origin conflicts are intensely acted out in the couple's realm with identifications and counter-identifications being quite common (Siegel 2004). This leads to outrageous reactions to everyday events or non-reactions to dramatic events. In the transference, couples see us as the one who will decide who is right and who is wrong. Then, we are expected to magically fix the problem in these firestorms of love and hate or they see us as letting them down and not helping.

During the more volatile moments of accusation and reaction, the analyst must often act as policeman and referee for the acting out that endangers the pathological organization. Once we stabilize the acting out, we can further help the couple by interpreting the mutual anxiety over the potential collapse of their well-known yet unhealthy system that they rely on for projective identification reassurance, gratification, and power. Only by working within that mutually constructed system of destructive delusional of false security and last-resort conflict resolution can we eventually offer the couple a way out and a new way of being together as well as apart.

At the same time, sudden shifts of analytic focus are often necessary. With the overwhelmed and chaotic couples we see, the analyst must often follow one or both parties as they flee from the pathological organization to their private psychic retreats. Consistent in-the-moment interpretive and containing work is vital to building the potential shift back to the couple's pathological organization. In other words, the one-to-one, here-and-now, moment-to-moment analytic work with both individuals is the only way to eventually find the opportunity to get back to work on the couple's issues and what historical matters have influenced both parties and the couple as a unit.

So, we can find ourselves traveling to and fro from the pathological organization to the individual psychic retreats and then back to the pathological organization. But hopefully, along the way, we help the couple build a gradual patchwork of new and healthier relational elements and a life-enhancing cycle of projective identification that reinforces change, acceptance, and difference.

With couples rooted in pathological organizations and defensive psychic retreats, the transference material is often more apparent and intense between the two parties. Yet, even then, the analyst is often transformed into the ultimate idealized arbitrator of who is good or bad, a primitive parent figure and quick-fix doctor who will do the dirty work for the couple so that they can quickly return to the safety and denial of the pathological organization. Couples in this state of psychological disorganization tend to act out a great deal, bringing a sharp focus on the interpersonal and impulsive or immature behavioral patterns (Sander 2004).

In such clinical situations, the analyst must strive to bring this externalized way of living back to the internal, helping the couple become curious about the inner basis of their troubles. This is of course an uphill task, since knowledge about self and other is considered dangerous and akin to loss of control, power, and love.

Dougherty (1997) has noted how successful long-term relationships require a tolerance for the otherness of the object. The troubled and turbulent couple end up involved in pathological bargains with each other (Waska 2005) and restricted to a one-dimensional projective identification system or pathological organizations that bypass the necessary elements of otherness.

In healthy couples, the life instinct promotes respect for difference and love of need and change; but, if the ancient repetition of particular self and object transferences in more pathological couples is disrupted or in peril due to difference, need, change, or growth, the death instinct begins to overshadow their relationship (Segal 1993). This is the defensive destruction of desire, dependence, difference, learning, and knowledge so that the familiar sameness, the known match or mismatch, can continue to recycle for eternity without question. This is part of the therapeutic crossroads, resistance, and impasse we encounter in couples treatment.

The couple will rely on the components of the death instinct as the principal aspect of their projective identification-based pathological organization in order to regain psychic equilibrium (Joseph 1989; Spillius and Feldman 1989; Steiner 1992) or they will flee to private psychic retreats (Steiner 1993) where they see their partner as a foe who challenges the status quo and causes pain and uncertainty. Likewise, one or both parties may see the analyst in this way and unite in the pathological organization with the death instinct as their mutual vehicle to combat the specter of the analyst.

So, our usual analytic work to liberate new and creative objects and healthy ways of viewing the self is often seen as simply a threat to the balance or existence of the pathological organization and sometimes even to the private psychic retreats. Nevertheless, we make observations (Waska 2012) and interpretations to help the couple question their relationship which in turn allows them to create new possibilities. However, the more disturbed couple experiences this as a taking away of what is safe and known and being forced to deal with what is unknown and unfamiliar. This exposes vulnerability, need, and lack of control, all quite unbearable to patients suffering in more paranoid-schizoid or pre-depressive modes. Therefore, we must then interpret these anxieties and help the couple through this traumatic transition to healing, change, and growth.

Many couples being seen in today's private practice settings are mired in a primitive zone of paranoid and narcissistic functioning without any access to the internal vision of a pleasurable object with which to merge without catastrophe. Feeling securely grounded is voided and feeling emotionally buried in the ground is ever present. These are couples who both defend against the more erotic, pleasurable, and connective elements of relationship as well as against their fears of conflict, aggression, and growth.

The clinical approach of Modern Kleinian Therapy includes the constant awareness of how the couple, individually or together, may be trying to deny, delay, decay, or destroy the intimacy, truthfulness, and vulnerability that analytic work creates, demands, and discovers. Through projective identification-based transference attacks, the analyst may come to feel this doubt and dread.

This chapter views Kleinian psychoanalytic technique, as practiced both by classical Kleinians such as Hanna Segal (1981, 1997) and refined by contemporary Kleinians (Schafer 2000) such as Betty Joseph (1978, 1982, 1983, 1988) and Michael Feldman (1992, 2004, 2009) to be transferable to low-frequency cases, to couples therapy, and to work with more disturbed borderline, narcissistic, and psychotic patients.

In broadening Klein's work to match today's clinical climate, Modern Kleinian Therapy makes use of Kleinian technique to work with couples facing severe relational crises. As with individual psychoanalytic treatment, the analyst is always attempting to engage the couple in an exploration of their unconscious phantasies, transference patterns, defenses, and internal experience of the world. The goal of understanding unconscious phantasy, the resolution of intra-psychic conflict, and the integration of self–object relations, both internally and externally, is the same with couples. The psychoanalyst uses interpretation as the principal tool, and transference, counter-transference, and projective identification are the three clinical guideposts of those interpretive efforts (Hinshelwood 1999, 2004; Hargreaves and Varchenker 2004; Joseph 1985; Waska 2007, 2010b, 2013).

Viewed from the Kleinian perspective, most couples utilize projective identification as a psychic cornerstone for defense, communication, attachment, learning, loving, and aggression (Waska 2010c, 2010d, 2011b). As such, projective identification constantly shapes and colors both the transference and counter-transference as well as defining the type of pathological organization the couple depends on for psychic equilibrium.

Couples work is inherently more difficult than individual work, as the analyst is always faced with the dynamics of the couple as well as the individual psychological make-up of each party. Successful analytic contact with couples involves not only psychic change, but a corresponding sense of loss and mourning. Every moment, analytic contact is both an experience of hope and transformation as well as dread and despair as the couple struggle with change. They face a new way of being with each other and with themselves. Successful analytic work always results in a cycle of fearful risk taking, hasty retreats, retaliatory attacks, anxious detours, and attempts to shift the treatment into something less than analytic, something less painful.

The analyst's interpretations of these reactions to the precarious journey of growth are meant to be a way of steering the treatment back to something more analytic, something that contains more meaningful contact with self and other. The support we give the couple includes the inherent vow that we will help them survive this painful contact and walk with them into the unknown. This unknown involves giving up the pathological organization for the chance to find or build something new for each other, and the risk of being open with each other in a new way unbound by projective identification patterns means being open with each other without the unconscious back-up plan of being able to flee back to their individual psychic retreats.

Of course, this is all a matter of degree. All relationships involve some element of psychic retreat and pathological organization, but analytic couples treatment seeks to minimize it in favor of more fulfilling and healthy ways of relating and coping.

Modern Kleinian Therapy fosters this potential establishment of analytic contact (Waska 2007), but facilitates the patient's psychological investment in an analytic relationship or a relational link that allows for mutual exploration, learning, curiosity, growth, and change. The analyst observes how the patient reacts to this opportunity and the resulting level of engagement, retreat, defense, or attack on the potential analytic contact. When analytic contact is avoided, eliminated, or perverted, it is often the result of the defensive use of the death instinct and the accompanying excessive projective identification processes.

In Modern Kleinian Therapy, interpretations are made as soon as either party or the couple presents a transference effort, be that aggressive, loving, exploratory, or indifferent. While some psychoanalytic approaches wait for the patient to bring up their feelings regarding conflict or advocate supportive and mirroring, all techniques for what the analyst believes to be a damaged or defective ego state (Ruggiero 2012), Modern Kleinian Therapy operates with the underpinning that careful and thoughtful interpretation or observation (Waska 2012) of any and all conflicts with love, hate, or knowledge is the most supportive and attentive action one can take. In addition, while some couples or individuals react with anxiety or retreat to this interpretive focus, it serves to offer the necessary containment needed, especially early on in the treatment with the more chaotic and brittle borderline or narcissistic couple.

This approach is even more helpful and therapeutically necessary with couples because of the increased level of acting out and constant emotional lack of balance seen in couples whose trusted illusion of control vanishes when the pathological organization breaks down and their regular state of psychic equilibrium has collapsed.

Case material

Ann and Bill came into couples treatment two years ago. At that time, they were unable to communicate effectively with each other because of their turbulent, intense, and destructive cycles of projective identification. Instead, they operated within a pathological organization (Steiner 1987) with predictable and confining patterns of destructive attachment. This static and chaotic system brought them some security and gratification but was constantly breaking down, with each of them fleeing into private psychic retreats.

Neither Ann nor Bill had the ability to contain their persecutory anxieties and narcissistic impulses. Respectful limits towards each other or the couple were lacking or absent. On one hand, they felt drawn to each other by shared views in life and many similar interests. In addition, they felt they had found a welcome respite in each other from the conflicts they grew up with.

However, these areas of familiarity were also the battlefield for severe verbal fights and occasional physical fights. Ann and Bill have had many crippling life experiences and they both have highly conflicted internal phantasy states that currently affect them individually and mutually. We are working through these relational impasses, so typical of pathological organizations and their breakdown as well as their individual psychic retreats. While the work is slow and rocky, much progress has been made.

In fact, over the past six months there have been many moments in which I have been able to engage with both Ann and Bill as a couple, rather than having to work with them one at a time when they are hiding out in their psychic retreats. They are more often existing in their pathological organization in which there are threads of genuine caring and life-enhancing connection woven around a very rigid and stagnant way of non-relating and provocation.

Primarily, this pathological organization is a system of projective identification patterns loyal to the death instinct aspect of their shared psychology. Difference, need, separation, and the unknown aspects of self and other are all targets for neutralization. Ann and Bill are dedicated to narrowly defined roles with each other, both interpersonally and intra-psychically. These sets of predictable dysfunction create ongoing tension that eventually escalates until this unstable match breaks down. Then, they have to flee to their private psychic retreats. However, they have both been able to notice this escalation of the destructive and defensive aspects of the death instinct operating in their relationship and have been successful in finding ways of de-escalating. They are assuming more responsibility for what and how they each contribute to this cycle. These moments provide breakthroughs into more depressive position and whole-object functioning as well as a new, healthier harmony in which life-affirming patterns of projective identification are possible. This is the important transition from pathological organization to healthy unity.

In the process of working through the elements of their pathological organization, Ann and Bill still often flee back to their private psychic retreats to gain control and root themselves in denial and narcissistic righteousness. In helping each of them through the more personal anxieties that make up these psychic retreats, we have dealt with certain early family experiences and the ongoing repetition of these dynamics, both internally and externally, in the transference, and in the couple's bond. The more we were able to understand, contain, and translate their individual phantasies and conflicts, the more they were able to return to the leaky raft of their pathological organization. Once there, we were again in the position of working out some of their fundamental struggles with each other as a couple. This opens up the opportunity for the positive life-affirming cycles of healing projective identification cycles that hold healthy couples together in flexible and accepting ways that allow for difference, autonomy, and unity.

Bill is a middle-aged scientist who prides himself on being smart, responsible, and intelligent. He believes in doing everything to its most productive, efficient, by-the-book, best-possible manner. So, even his hobbies are very controlled like a science experiment, focused and something he wants to excel at. Bill tells me there is a proper method to do everything and "it's all about execution, timing, and study. If you do it properly, you get the most out of it." He might use this phrase to describe his passion for bowling.

At the beginning of their relationship, this was something Ann was drawn to. She respected Bill for being punctual, determined, and defined, all characteristics missing from her early childhood experiences and things she struggled with in her adult life. But, later on in the relationship, she felt that Bill was controlling, obsessive, and mean. She described him demanding that she always excel at anything they did, so there could never be any lazy, fun, and non-deliberate time spent together. In response, Bill would tell me how unfocused, mercurial, and lacking in purpose she was, "a real threat to my life and my life goals."

As is the case with many couples, there was some truth in both of their accusations of each other but the real problems came from the projective identification distortions and exaggerations that now made up the pathological organization and allowed for no change and no challenge to the status quo.

As a child, Ann did not have a chance to become involved in her school work due to her abusive family environment. As a result, she never found herself feeling comfortable in academic settings. So, Ann was initially very interested in being with Bill because of his intellect and his academic interests. But Bill openly says that he wishes he was with someone of "equal intellect" so that he can have "interesting and stimulating conversations." This is a repeat of Bill's experience of being made his mother's peer in her rambling conversations with him as a child. She treated him as if he was an adult and a friend with whom she could have lengthy talks about politics, sex, and philosophy. This made Bill feel important and powerful, but unaware of how he was being used by his mother.

When Bill is verbally demeaning to Ann, she does not say much about how it hurts her feelings. Instead, she starts a fight about the more concrete aspects of Bill's putdown. This ignoring of her feelings is a repeat of when Ann felt put down and devalued as a child but could not stand up for herself or share her feelings safely with anyone. She told me, "it was wrong for Bill to not respect me" but then she switched to somehow agreeing that he was the smart one and she was somehow lacking. I interpreted that it was hard for her to look to me or to Bill for validation of her worth and hard for her to respect herself sometimes. Ann said, "I don't know what I have to offer except for sex." I said, "You don't think your mind and heart are worth much. No one would love you for that." She said, "That can be a problem sometimes!"

An illustration of their dynamics is as follows. Bill would come home from work and start to tell Ann about some complex topic he was thinking about, usually politics or science. He expected her to be able to join him on his level and basically be "an academic debater or share elements of value on the same playing field." When she did not, Bill told her that she was "stupid and lacking in creative intelligence." He told her he was worried about "not having the intellectual equal in my life I feel I deserve."

Ann was hurt by these remarks and this often led to horrible arguments, with one of them walking out of the house. Bill could not really see the sheer arrogance and emotional violence of his comments. Often, in turn, Ann would call him an "emotional retard who is never willing to talk about anything." Indeed, she felt he was so unavailable emotionally that they often ended up in terrible fights after she "wanted to talk about her feelings" or wanted to "talk about the relationship" and he would tell her he was busy reading or surfing the internet. She would feel rejected and persist in asking him to talk about things. He felt pressured and cornered by this and told me,

> she ends up talking all night long about useless crap. She wants to talk about how we should communicate better or how she felt upset over her day at work. She never stops. It just goes on and on. She is very selfish that way and can't seem to know how to just keep it to herself or to not take everything so personally.

This would also infuriate Ann and she would feel "hopeless about the relationship" and bring up how she needed to find other men with whom to share her feelings. This of course made Bill anxious and jealous and he would lash out verbally.

In fact, Bill was often sure she might be cheating on him. So, he tried to control her with threats, restrict her to having no contact with other men, or sought revenge on her by going to prostitutes "to deal with his anxiety."

Bill was in fact overwhelmed by anxiety and depression much of the time, feeling he was not living up to his own expectations for greatness and feeling unable to control Ann. He felt she was volatile and unpredictable, and he "never knew when she might talk to her old boyfriend." So, Bill feared losing control and having no predictability along with feeling that there were no safe limits upon which to depend. His worries about Ann's old boyfriend and other men she might "hook up with" were connected to how Ann had been a call girl for several years. When they met, he found this sexy and attractive but now saw it as a threat. For years, Ann had also maintained a perverse daddy/daughter sexual relationship with an older married man. Now, and throughout their relationship, she would call him whenever she wanted to "have a meaningful emotional discussion about things with someone who cares about my feelings and understands where I came from." Whenever I or Bill brought up the problematic nature of her continuing to see him given this sexual affair history and the perverse nature of the bond to begin with, Ann usually brushed our concerns aside as silly or old-fashioned.

Bill was also often upset about "how she always changes our plans." He felt angry about Ann altering plans they had talked about or suggesting new ideas that seemed to come "out of the blue." I talked with Bill about how he seemed to obsessively lock into the security of knowing exactly what the schedule was going to be so that any possible change or disruption felt very threatening and out of his control. In the transference, I interpreted to Bill that when he didn't know where I was going with a given line of questions he also became irritated and anxious. He wanted to know exactly what my plans for the session were and what my agenda for him or both of them was at any given moment. Otherwise, he felt I was withholding, possibly manipulating him, or perhaps not really knowing what I was doing, since I didn't seem to have a specific plan.

Bill also became angry and anxious if he couldn't have what he wanted when he wanted it. As an example, when he was causing a great deal of turmoil in the relationship with his heavy pot smoking and drinking, Ann asked him to stop. In response, Bill felt she was trying to control him and "take away my pleasures that belong to me." He felt she was not respecting his life and what he wanted to do with it. He felt she was nagging him and pressuring him, which would lead to more arguments and fights. Ann was close to leaving him on several occasions because of this and he said he would rather have her leave than for him to have to give up what he enjoyed. Rather than these examples being rare moments of crisis within a generally stable and healthy relationship, they were more of an ongoing pattern that made up the pathological organization, a system of projective identification attacks and defensive moves that comprised the fabric of their lives together.

Bill's sense of entitlement, persecution, and intolerance started to make more sense when we explored his upbringing. He described a significant lack of boundaries between him and his mother. On one hand, she spoiled him and told him he was an exceptional person who was far smarter than all the other children and destined for greatness. Bill's parents divorced when he was ten and he openly wept, describing how he missed his father and felt he had "missed out on the chance to have someone teach him how to be a man and guide him through life."

I interpreted that he had possibly combined his mother's inflated view of him with his own childish notions of what a man should be and was left with a grandiose image of himself. I added that he had no father to balance that out and to show him the limits of things, and the realistic ways in which to view himself and others. Bill agreed and told me he finds himself "searching for a roadmap in life that I think my father could have given me."

When he was a child and a teenager, Bill's mother used him as a friend and confidant, scrutinizing all his friends and girlfriends. This continued into his adult life where she lectured him on his relationship with Ann. She told him Ann was not smart or pretty enough for him and asked him for details of their sex life. Bill went ahead and told her what she wanted to know, seeming to think nothing of it.

I spent much time with Bill exploring this complete lack of boundaries and the ways it made him feel close and special to his mother, but how it also controlled him and subjected him to a frightening and perverse lack of limits. I interpreted that this may have been part of what drew him to Ann in the first place, since Ann also had a history of no boundaries. But now, Bill simply felt that Ann was going to hurt him or dull his life with her lack of knowledge and limits. I pointed out that he was in fact hurting her and the relationship by allowing his mother into their bedroom and into their lives by sharing all this information with his mother. In addition, I pointed out how he was very anxious and angry that Ann was going to do this very same thing with her friends and her married ex-boyfriend. He was doing what his mother did with him but he wasn't letting himself see the parallel. After working on this for months, Bill brought in an email from his mother. He said he and Ann had both felt the email was "a bit over the top" and wanted to discuss it.

In the email, Bill's mother referred to the ways in which she felt "most people make bad parents" and gave several examples of how various friends were not "doing things right." She added that she hoped that if Bill were to have children he would make sure Ann understood the importance of good child-rearing. She went on to mention something about Ann and Bill's sex life regarding what positions they used and I asked how she would know such details. Bill said casually that she had asked about their sex life a year before and he had told her the details. He said he "realized it was probably not a great idea but she asked." The main reason Bill and Ann brought the email in was their concern over how Bill's mother might be a controlling influence if and when they did have children. They both seemed to ignore the sexual invasiveness part of it and left me to be the one to bring it up.

I said I thought they were both wanting to use me as the one who needed to raise a red flag about how over the top Bill's mother was and to be the one who questioned both of them as to why they didn't see the whole thing, including the sex issue, as inappropriate. In other words, in their pathological organization, they were in agreement about the concrete threat of Bill's mother being controlling if they had children. But this unconscious agreement shielded both of them from having to look at how they individually and together denied the complete lack of boundaries that was apparent. It seemed that no one felt comfortable looking around and questioning how few limits there were between people until it felt suffocating and overwhelming, and led to a fight. This was happening in the transference at that moment in their lack of awareness about the strange sexual overlap between Bill and his mother. How that directly affected their privacy and intimacy was projected on to me. I was to be the one who voiced the problem, stirred up conflict, and set limits. I interpreted this to be comfortable for them so that they didn't have to incorporate this new way of living and relating into their relationship.

Bill and Ann's mutual denial of the healthy balance between personal need and respecting the other's needs was not much of a surprise, given how they both had a history of trouble with limits, boundaries, and identity definition. As mentioned above, Bill had grown up with his mother clearly overstepping her role with him, sharing sexual secrets with him, and generally controlling him. Bill described being used emotionally and sexually through her verbal intrusiveness and with her pushy opinions about who was good or bad and what was right or wrong. These issues had then developed into ways Bill mistreated Ann and saw their relationship in certain static and problematic ways.

For Ann, a lack of limits was also a familiar way of living. She grew up in a very strict and abusive environment. Her father was a hard-drinking man with a "terrible temper that often meant some form of violence." Ann was molested by her father from the age of eleven to fifteen. We have understood the impact of this traumatic childhood as shaping her decision to be a call girl in her twenties and her long-term affair with a married man who cast himself in the role of "daddy" and treated Ann as a young girl whom he was "mentoring."

Throughout her relationship with Bill, Ann has had many "slips" in which she has gone back to that man. I have interpreted these slips as a way of getting back at him when she felt hurt and angry. What has made their relationship even more problematic was how in the beginning of the relationship they both agreed to possibly see other people. However, whenever that actually occurred, they both felt it was part of an angry betrayal that was already in the air and now simply acted out. Then they would fight and both would feel lied to and manipulated.

Overall, I interpreted how they both felt they wanted to be above limits and felt they deserved a special freedom. For Bill, I interpreted that he wanted to do as he pleased to break out of the control he felt internally from his mother; but he also felt entitled to this because of how she treated him like a king. For Ann, I interpreted that she wanted to break free of her father's rigid and dominating control to do her own thing in life, but ended up acting out the same sadomasochistic and perverted relating she experienced in her family, only now she was both the perpetrator and the victim.

I interpreted that they both felt strongly drawn to each other by the idea that they could have this special freedom and be themselves in a new way that transcended their difficult past and their internal restrictions on self. This was the great promise of the pathological organization to which they remained loyal, but this phantasy of special freedom often got out of hand and each felt threatened by the other's desire for freedom to do as they pleased without limits or consideration of the other. This led to each withdrawing to their psychic retreats.

I also interpreted that their individual transference distortions of the other led to severe reactions and acting out. So, for Bill, he saw Ann as an irritating dumb person whom he needed to educate and control, and he felt he had to look out for her threatening tendency to hurt him and betray him by seeing other men. Underneath this, he saw her as a replica of his mother, someone who was intrusive, never respectful of his privacy, and possibly ready to hurt him with a lack of sexual boundaries. For Ann, she saw Bill an arrogant bully, someone who could hurt her physically but more so hurt her emotionally by always denying her the love, understanding, and closeness she craved, all a repeat of her father's abuse and neglect.

During several recent sessions, Bill and Ann came in and asked me to help them decide what the "normal way is" regarding a new area of conflict. In the past, when Bill was drunk, smoking lots of pot, or having a temper outburst, she would immediately contact one of her friends and tell them all about the incident. This might be a man but also some of her girlfriends. In doing so, Bill felt that Ann was always painting him in a bad light and being impulsive about how quickly she shared things, not allowing them "to maybe work it out naturally between ourselves."

In response, Ann felt very uncomfortable "being limited to not sharing" because for many years she would either share everything about her current life situation with friends or she would anonymously post it online in a blog. Ann felt "lost" without that "outlet." Bill felt she was "betraying their trust and relationship" and "not allowing him to have any choice in the matter." He said "she was controlling it all." So, we were exploring the familiar themes that they both grappled with: issues of limits, boundaries, trust, power, control, and dependency.

In examining this situation, Ann told me about her anxieties over not being able to "tell someone about what he is doing to me." I clarified that while they did have a history of getting into awful fights that were sometimes violent and Bill could be very mean and verbally abusive to her, the way she said it sounded like as if she was reliving some very traumatic moment with her father and she wanted to tell someone about it and get help. She thought about it and said she "could see that." She went on to associate how when Bill gets angry she immediately thinks of how he "will throw me against the refrigerator." I asked if this might also be a memory of her father or whether Bill had resorted to this type of violence before. Ann was quick to say, "Oh no. Bill may have a temper but he has never done anything like that and I can't picture him ever doing that. But, my father did that to me several times. So, I guess I am thinking more about that than what he is doing."

I added,

> So when you want to run to a friend and tell them what you are up against, it sounds like you want someone to talk to about these horrible memories of being molested and beaten, not someone to tell the details of your current argument with Bill. Maybe it might help to talk more with Bill about these things, so you can really tell the difference between him and your father.

We went on to discuss the possibility of her talking about how he was scaring her and for them to help each other by separating their projections from reality. In doing so, they would be undoing the pathological organization and creating a new, healthier relationship based on reality and finally seeing who they really were for each other.

This line of thought continued with Bill. For him, we found out that the idea of Ann suddenly running to someone and telling them everything made him very anxious and angry because it felt like a repeat of the lack of limits he had with his mother, the way his mother controlled him, and how she "made everything about her." So, I interpreted how he was more comfortable doing battle with the specter of his mother by seeing Ann as the very same than to have to work on those internal conflicts as his own and to have to relate to Ann as a separate person on her own with her own set of characteristics that he could not so easily predict, control, or judge without also having to look at his own contribution to the mix.

In the next session, this exploration continued. Bill told me he "resents how if Ann thinks we are having a problem, we have to stop and talk about it. Then, we talk about our relationship forever. Meanwhile, whatever we are doing is put on hold and we never accomplish anything." He went on to give me an example that happened the day before. Ann and Bill had bought a new computer and were working together to set it up in their home. At some point, Ann asked him to hand her a cable and called it "the long plug-in thing." Bill became angry and told her she was stupid for not knowing to call it by its proper name. Ann said she didn't think it was wrong to call it by her shorthand name, to which Bill repeated his opinion of her as dumb and not aware of commonplace information. They argued for a while about this.

I interpreted that they were both very comfortable staying on the level of these concrete matters: names for items. This was part of the security of the pathological organization. They were both insecure about being aware of and discussing their feelings about the meaning of the debate. Bill said it makes him uneasy to realize he is with someone who is not very smart. He feels he is without an equal partner. Ann said she doesn't like to be abused and threatened. Here, I interpreted that both of them were acting out early and familiar mismatched bonds with their parents and using their relationship as a way to continuously replay various struggles, wishes, and fears they did not want to face and own. Instead, they projected and disowned them.

So, Bill would devalue his object much like his mother did to everyone around her and then he would feel surrounded by incompetence. This made him anxious and angry. "There is no efficiency and no intellectual satisfaction," he would yell. Bill felt trapped by Ann's desire to "talk about the relationship." He pictured how all his goals and projects were now on hold until he went through her "relentless discussion of feelings." So, in the pathological organization, she was a dumb object who intruded her needs onto him without respecting his limits or need for privacy. His needs and goals were forfeited for this selfish object's demands.

For Ann, I interpreted that in the pathological organization she had a volatile, controlling object that didn't respect her. Her only options were to either get him to explain his motives and apologize or to act out sexually to gain control and revenge.

I interpreted that in this endless projective identification cycle that makes up the couple's pathological organization, there is always hope for change but the anxiety and the defensive reactions to the dangers of change prevent the hope from ever coming to fruition. Instead, the projective identification distortions simply become overwhelming at some point, forcing them to flee to their psychic retreats. But I interpreted that, despite the endless conflict and avoidance of change, they are also genuinely wanting some new form of relating. For Bill, he hopes to find respect and healthy sharing. For Ann, she hopes to find trust and safe expression of self.

Currently, we continue to work towards this change and hope. Using their fight over their computer as an example, we discussed how it might be if they both gave up their usually rigid and controlling projective identification defenses that combine to form the pathological organization. With my prompting, we came to see that one possibility, a more forgiving and whole-object experience, might be that Bill could see Ann's lack of knowledge about the cable as a "silly way she can be" or "something that endears her to him." They could still be partners who work effectively together even though each person does not have exactly the same knowledge or skill as the other. In other words, difference is not something to attack and not something that will cause hurt or failure. The death instinct need not be the driving force of their bond. Bill said that this sort of thinking was "something I want to learn more about, but I think I have a way to go."

Again with my prompting, Ann said she could imagine

> seeing Bill as super geeky, someone who gets really into these projects and temporarily forgets about everything else. He has feelings but like a little boy he gets scared to let them out. But, if I give him some space and ask nicely, sometimes he is willing to come out and play.

So, Ann was thinking about tolerating Bill's absence as a good object without feeling threatened and she was thinking about forgiveness and acceptance, since the trouble was "only temporary." Like Bill, she was "not there yet," but we are on our way.

Discussion

In the more primitive and paranoid climate of pathological organizations which we typically encounter in couples treatment, the absence of a good object is experienced as the presence of a bad object, and the recognition of whole objects with both good and bad qualities culminating in ambivalence is unbearable. Coming to terms with the separateness of the primary object requires the experience of mourning which is beyond the capacity of most couples starting analytic treatment. Therefore, we try to help the couple navigate through their conflict and anxiety so that they may reach more whole-object functioning.

However, the first phase of the depressive position (Klein 1935, 1940) is dominated by the fear of loss and this fuels a desire to preserve the object at any cost, including the denial of the reality of loss. Here the temporary loss of the other through change, difference, or growth is experienced as a personal and permanent death, not as unbearable as the threat of annihilation in the paranoid-schizoid position but almost as catastrophic. In more mature and stable moments, loss involves acknowledging the object as separate. To allow the object its independence, one must accept that the object cannot be protected or controlled. Again, the pathological organization protects the couple from these fears and narcissistic blows, but keeps them frozen in their mutual stagnation and projective-based anxieties. If the pathological organization breaks down, one or both parties will resort to withdrawal into psychic retreats. Steiner (1990, 1992) contends that psychic retreats serve to interfere with the achievement of mourning, particularly the realization of the object as separate and out of one's control. Again, this has to do with the anxieties and conflicts regarding the workings of the life-and-death instincts.

When projective identification becomes an established and over-relied-upon form of interaction with objects, it can lead to a belief, either illusory or real, that the object is under one's possession, securely controlled (Steiner 1989; Waska 2004, 2006, 2010a, 2011a). With couples, this can bring about a calm sense of trust – "we are on the same page" – a feeling of like-mindedness, and a sense of common purpose. In healthy relating, a certain amount of this is normal and helpful; but, when excessive and fueled by various aggressive, guilt-ridden, or persecutory motives, it creates a false sense of trust and harmony that masks ongoing pain and dysfunction. In this situation, unless the projective control and possession can be relinquished and mourning for the lost object worked through, a more chronic and almost permanent form of projective identification develops as a defense against separateness (Rosenfeld 1964, 1971). This is the essence of pathological organizations in couples. The internal situation often becomes highly structured and object relationships are bound into complex networks described in detail by Rosenfeld (1971) that provide an unhealthy stability or psychic equilibrium that is resistant to change.

Pathological organizations fluctuate in intensity and, when expected projective identification experiences fail to materialize, one or both parties escape to their psychic retreats until they elect to risk returning to their normal level of mutual pathological psychic equilibrium. We usually see couples at either the height of the pathological organization's dysfunction, decay, or breakdown, or we meet the couple at a point where both parties have barricaded themselves into individual psychic retreats. Often, we have to deal with the sealed-off, defended emotional fortress of each party's psychic retreat before the couple can emerge in a more engaged posture. However, it is rare that either or both parties are then available to begin working through their conflicts.

Indeed, they are usually more apt to re-establish their pre-existing pathological organizations and to continue their prior mutual defensive, fixed, and destructive state of projective identification equilibrium. As the analyst begins working on this mutual state of static chaos, it is common for the parties to again feel overwhelmed now by the analyst, feeling that their mutual equilibrium is again in danger. So, they elect to seek refuge once again in their individual psychic retreats or to pit the mutual pathological organization against the perceived threat of the analyst which usually results in abrupt acting out and sudden terminations.

Much of the work with couples and their defensive insistence upon not shifting their reliance onto the pathological organization or the psychic retreat has to do with projective identification issues and problems of containment. Emergence from both the psychic retreat and the pathological organization means having to face psychic reality and involves a relinquishment of the object, its role as container, and an experience of total unity. When this necessary loss and confrontation with reality is too much to bear, the individual may either withdraw back into their psychic retreat or return to the refuge of the pathological organization.

Regarding the necessary loss of the object as container, Steiner (1990, 1996) has noted two stages. In the first stage, the object is used as a container to collect, integrate, and give meaning to disparate parts of the self. Bion (1962) suggested that it is through being understood in this way that the projections become more acceptable to the patient, who can take them back in a modified form. In Steiner's view however, containment temporarily relieves anxiety and provides a sense of being understood but does not in itself permit a true separateness to be achieved. Indeed, with couples, they often require each other to be hostages, permanently kidnapped and used as containers for all unwanted emotional conflict and to create the illusion of the fulfillment of all primitive wishes and demands. If they fail to be this perfect container, it may trigger the partner into narcissistic entitlement, paranoid fears, and justified rage. This is the point where the pathological organization breaks down and psychic retreats are utilized for aggressive defense.

Steiner has noted that it is not until projections are fully withdrawn that the vital work of mourning is possible. For many couples, the death instinct is at its peak during this troubled time in the relationship, as a way to eliminate mourning, difference, separation, or loss. In the pathological organization, the patient internalizes an object containing parts of the self still inextricably bound to it by force, and the loss of the object during actual or phantasized separations is denied by a phantasy of omnipotent possession of it. The relief from anxiety comes from a sense of being understood by the partner and relies on the partner's authority or the control of the partner. Thus, we see sadomasochistic relating in many of the more troubled couples. Understanding as opposed to being understood has to arise from within and depends on a capacity to think and judge for oneself. Therefore, it involves a relinquishment of a dependence on the views and judgments of the partner or the analyst.

Such a relinquishment ushers in the second phase, which represents a move towards independence and towards facing the pain of separation and difference. Again, this may be the beginning of a mutual reliance upon the life instinct, the relinquishment of the pathological organization for a more loving, realistic relationship without guarantee or control but full of wonderful surprise and enhancement through difference, change, negotiation, and parallel growth.

Part IV

Character structure as portrayed in film

Chapter 9

Another fear and another tear

Psychoanalytic considerations of the film *Another Year*

In this chapter, the Kleinian psychoanalytic concepts of paranoid-schizoid, depressive position, containment, envy, and the death instinct will be used to explore the unconscious dynamics at work in the film *Another Year*. Specifically, the need for a reliable psychological container to make the developmental transition from paranoid-schizoid functioning to depressive position functioning is explored by looking at the relationship between two of the film's main characters.

The Kleinian perspective

Throughout life, the subject projects their various feelings and thoughts about self and other onto their valued or despised object and then internalizes the combination of reality and their distortion back inside. This starts another cycle of unconscious coping and reaction to that new internal object which is then projected again. Thus, there is a never-ending recycling of one's vision of self and other that one is continuously organizing, relating, and reacting to, both externally and internally as well as intra-psychically and interpersonally. In the paranoid-schizoid position, these internal objects are often fragmented part objects rather than the more integrated whole objects experienced in the depressive position.

In the more immature, primitive state of mind that Melanie Klein termed the paranoid-schizoid, objects and the self are experienced in one-dimensional, black-and-white manners that involve splitting and more rudimentary functioning. This state of mind is dominated by projective identification and splitting, and leaves the subject feeling persecuted and abandoned by bad objects or united with and loved by idealized objects. The paranoid-schizoid mode is usually found in more borderline, narcissistic, or psychotic patients but we all exist within this mode to some degree or can easily regress to it under trying circumstances. Klein believed the healthy transition from the paranoid-schizoid experience to more whole-object depressive functioning had much to do with the constitutional balance of the life-and-death instincts and the external conditions of optimal mothering. The primary anxiety in this position has to do with survival of the self rather than concern for the object.

The depressive position is the realm of psychological experience discovered by Klein and characterized by the realization of dependent and hateful feelings towards the loved object, producing guilt and fear of loss. As opposed to earlier paranoid phantasies of ideal and loved objects versus other, more persecutory and hated objects, now the subject faces the difficult reality of whole objects towards which one has a variety of feelings. This creates ambivalence, anxiety, and the desire to repair, restore, and rescue the injured other. Anxiety is still about the survival of the self if abandoned or punished by the offended and hurt object, but now the anxiety is much more about the well-being of the object. Obsessive and manic defenses come into play, and projective identification phantasies are much more about the relationship to the object as opposed to the stark division of self and other found in the paranoid position.

Kleinian theory holds envy to be a constitutional manifestation of the death instinct and gratitude a constitutional manifestation of the life instinct. Envy often surfaces around feelings of being without, not included, or of not having the valuable attributes of the other. Envy seeks to spoil or destroy what the other possesses, which is different than greed, in which one hopes to take away the object's treasures and have them for oneself. While envy seeks to take away the thing the other has, the anger involved makes it less about taking it and more about spoiling it or preventing it. Often, these patients have experienced great neglect and sometimes abuse, leaving them very conflicted about the good object and the goodness of that object (Waska 2005, 2007). They desperately want what the object has but are so angry and hurt about being excluded, rejected, or forgotten that they long to attack and destroy the treasures they want so much. This of course creates a vicious cycle and increases anxieties of both paranoid and depressive sorts. These issues are seen in the film's character of Mary, with her constantly feeling excluded, wanting what she feels is being withheld, and attacking her objects and their value in response.

The Kleinian notion of the container and the contained (Bion 1962; Cartwright 2010; Feldman 2009; Hargreaves and Varchenker 2004) is a concept of how certain conflicts, desires, fears, or gratitude are projected into the object with the hope of containment and possibly understanding or detoxification with an eventual returning of the reformed, solved, or translated material to the owner. The maternal container must be open and receptive, or the sender feels kept out and alone with unbearable internal anxiety. The basic function of the analyst interpreting is a model of receiving, containing, modifying, translating, and returning that provides the patient with this fundamental infant/mother experience. There are many ways in which this container/contained cycle can fail, be perverted, or put to the test during the patient's early family experiences as well as in the transference situation.

The modern clinical view of the life-and-death instincts involve Melanie Klein's modification of Freud's view of the two sides of the human condition. Modern Kleinian Therapy considers it vital to be aware of and engaged with the distinct anti-life and anti-growth or change force that seems to have an upper hand in some patients. The death instinct seems to arise most violently in situations of envy, difference, separation, or challenge to enduring pathological organizations (Rosenfeld 1987; Steiner 1993) and pathological forms of psychic equilibrium (Joseph 1989). Hanna Segal (1993, 1997) has defined it as the individual's reactions to needs. Either one can seek satisfaction for the needs, and accept and deal with the frustrations and problems that come with those efforts. This is life-affirming action or the actions of the life instinct. It is life-promoting and object-seeking. Eventually, this leads from concerns about the survival of the self to concerns about the well-being of the other.

The other reaction to needs is the drive to annihilate the self that has needs and to annihilate others and things that represent those needs. Kleinians see envy as a prime aspect of the death instinct, and early external experiences of deprivation and trauma play as much of a role as internal, constitutional factors in the ultimate balance between the life-and-death forces.

The film

Another Year is a 2010 British drama film written and directed by Mike Leigh, starring Lesley Manville as Mary, Jim Broadbent as Tom Hepple, and Ruth Sheen as Gerri Hepple. It premiered at the 2010 Cannes Film Festival and was nominated for an Academy Award as best original screenplay.

Tom Hepple is a geologist married to Gerri Hepple, a psychotherapy counselor. They are portrayed as an older married couple who have a comfortable, loving relationship but seemed surrounded by family and friends who all suffer marked unhappiness. The Hepples' only child, Joe, is thirty, unmarried, and works as a district attorney. He helps the poor with housing issues.

Gerri's long-time friend and colleague, Mary, works as a receptionist at the local health center. She is a middle-aged divorcee desperately wishing for a new relationship. She tells everyone she is happy but appears fraught with anxiety and is quite depressed. In addition, she is an alcoholic.

The film portrays many different times throughout the course of one year in which Mary and sometimes other friends are visiting the Hepple family. During these visits, the focus always ends up on the friends' most recent problems and emotional conflicts. Mary is the pivotal figure in these get-togethers and the one who always has some recent lament or crisis to announce. She is clingy, almost parasitic, in her quest for love, comfort, and companionship. She wants attention and is fast to weave complex sad stories about her misfortune for which she can receive understanding and reassurance.

No matter what, Mary finds a way to be the center of the stage, pulling on others to provide pity, love, and advice. When she is not able to have the object or person she wants, she becomes envious, pouty, resentful, and attacking. When Gerri's son, whom Mary pictures she could be with romantically, tells her he has a girlfriend, Mary becomes hurt and betrayed as well as vengeful and demanding.

Throughout the film, no one ever says no to Mary. She stumbles her way, literally and emotionally, into and through the Hepple family. Mary demands, begs, and manipulates them for love, acceptance, and pity. Over and over, Gerri and Tom tolerate her drunken, sobbing displays of despair. In fact, they seem to almost consider it a regular part of their life, never seeming to react or speak up. In this way, they enable Mary's behavior. Their tolerance or denial provides her with free passage to experience the world in a certain way, to relate to others in a certain way, and to view herself in a certain way. They help Mary to maintain her role as helpless and sad by providing no response or reaction. Everyone, including Mary, strives to put their best face on, to think of the positive side of things, and to see joy as just around the corner. Of course, this level of manic denial preserves the psychic equilibrium and saves Mary from ever facing the reality of her life.

Tom and Gerri seem to be happy in their marriage and are starting to face the reality of growing older. They talk with each other about how they too will soon be "part of history." They rejoice in memories of past trips and good times they used to have as well as looking forward to future vacations. They tend their community garden throughout the year, appreciating the experience even in the rain. In those moments, they seem to genuinely love life and benefit from being in it. They both show a strong degree of compassion towards, tolerance of, and forgiveness for their friend's problems, including Tom's alcoholic brother.

These are all healthy characteristics of depressive whole-object functioning (Spillius 1983, 1988, 1992; Spillius and Feldman 1989). However, Tom and Gerri both seem to always stop short of any conflict, difference, or independent voice when confronted with their friend's misery, self-sabotage, and destructive acting out. In this way, they both seem to avoid the messy, uncontrolled, and possibly hurtful aspects of the depressive position with its implied conflict, difference, and potential loss. At no time do they share their own advice, recommend change, or voice their displeasure. Unconditional love without displeasure, disapproval, critical concern, or disagreement is what they seem to embody, which is comparable to a welcoming and dry boat, but one that has no anchor. So, it can drift endlessly and aimlessly and never have a secure stance in a storm or ability to stand in one place for very long.

This seems equivalent to analytic patients who feel that their analysts "only listen and say nothing." While the psychoanalytic procedure is not about advice and direction, simple listening and acceptance alone can be felt as neglect or rejection. The act of interpretation is the manner in which we make verbal observations, confrontations, and suggested meaning to what seems formless or chaotic to the patient. Interpretation is our most powerful form of showing support, caring, and understanding. So, in that sense, Tom and Gerri seem happy and friendly on the surface, but also seem to not connect with their troubled friends. Instead of offering Mary any interpretive feedback or containment, they simply sit with Mary as she languishes within her state of crippling loss and emptiness (Bell 2011; Cartwright 2010; Steiner 2000; Waska 2002).

This type of artificial caring as a form of detachment that avoids conflict or uncertainty in the relationship creates a predictable, sad spiral. The Hepples simply observe their friend's misery but never engage in the situation to find or force deeper meaning. So, when Mary buys a car from two people who have obviously taken advantage of her, drives it while drunk, and begins to amass speeding and parking tickets as well as repair bills as it falls apart, Tom and Gerri say virtually nothing. Mary forces her trouble upon them verbally, emotionally, and interpersonally but they never respond, react, or push back. In this sense, Mary lacks any limits or containment from her objects.

In the latter part of the film, this dysfunctional method of being with Mary suddenly shifts. There are a few important moments in which Mary seems to respond very differently when finally confronted with an object that provides definition, difference, and limits through separate identity.

When Mary is driving a Hepple family friend and the Hepples' son back from a gathering, Mary becomes anxious and lonely and wants the son to stay with her. Even though she helped raise him and is now considered to be his aunt, Mary imagines they could be a loving couple. She begs him to stay with her and "tell her what to do, where to go, and how to be." He refuses and says he must go to sort out his own affairs. She is upset at not being able to have this symbiotic union, and confused by him wanting a separate identity away from her. She begs him some more and he still refuses. Afterwards, in the car, the family friend professes his love for Mary and, perhaps in response to being rejected by the son, Mary rejects the man. Later, Mary seems to quickly deny her sense of being unwanted by the son with more drinking.

But the reality of the son's autonomy and him demonstrating to Mary that he is not going to be forcibly connected or controlled by her occurs again when the son's new girlfriend comes to dinner at the Hepples. Mary has invited herself to dinner and, even though Gerri is visibly irritated, no one protests Mary's invasive nature or her drunken self-absorption. During dinner, Mary verbally devalues and attacks the son's new girlfriend. This intense envy and savage competition is brought to a halt, at least temporarily, when Gerri and her son tell Mary in a direct way that the son does indeed have a new girlfriend. They make a point to impress upon Mary that the son and the girl are a good match and are "serious" about their relationship. Gerri, in a surprising move of limit setting and object definition, reminds Mary that she is now considered "Auntie Mary" and seen as an older woman who was their helpful babysitter for Gerri's son. Mary is obviously hurt, crushed, and humiliated.

I believe this firm limit and definition of difference was a new form of containment that helped Mary to consider for a moment, and perhaps for the first time, herself as separate and different too. As a result, she had to suddenly face who she was, who she wasn't, what others had, and what she did not have in her life. This was her glimpse into the depressive world of whole real objects. Mary had to step away from the frantic, angry experience of overwhelming envy, desperate emotional hunger, and her borderline manner of refusing to grow up, to suddenly take in a moment of depressive position reflection. This brought with it enormous grief, loss, and psychic regret (Gold 1983; Grinberg 1964; Grotstein 2009).

Another pivotal moment in the film is when Mary comes over to the Hepple home unannounced following a drinking binge. She is depressed, and invading her objects in search of care, pity, and love. When Gerri sees her, Gerri expresses anger for one of the first times in their relationship. In fact, Gerri tells Mary, "I am disappointed with you." This creates a vivid reaction in Mary. She is immediately scared of the perceived abandonment, a sign of her paranoid-schizoid sense of catastrophic rejection as opposed to more mature depressive position fears of loss with survival possible (Joseph 1988).

Then, Mary tries to desperately assure Gerri that everything is okay, that she is very sorry, and that they are still friends. This is a manic and primitive maneuver to stop the terrifying rejection and force Gerri back into her control. It is not a real act of regret and reparation. Mary insists that "we are friends!" It is her insistence that speak to the control and aggressive demand to get things back to the usual level of psychic equilibrium.

It is at this point in the film that Gerri finally and fully emerges as a different form of container for Mary. She tells Mary that she must seek professional help. Mary reacts by saying she will simply talk to Gerri about her problems because they are already friends, so she doesn't need anyone else. Here, Mary is forcing the usual parasitic union and desperate love that prevents growth, difference, and healthy separation. But, finally, Gerri says no. She says, "We are friends but I can't help you. You need to see someone else." She says it as a differentiating limit and she stands her ground. Mary has to acknowledge it. There is a stunned silence. It seems that Mary is able or willing to take it in to some degree.

I believe Mary's interaction with this new container that Gerri provided, the "yes, we are still friends but —" container, allowed Mary to take a difficult but important step into the depressive position, at least for a moment. At the end of the film, after this jarring discussion with Gerri, Mary is having dinner with Tom, Gerri, their son, and his new girlfriend. Mary listens as they all talk about past memories of happy times, the happiness they have now, and the exciting plans they have for the future. The son talks about the joy of being a couple with his new girlfriend, and Tom and Gerri talk about their love for their son. They are all expressing independent and interdependent aspects of successful living, feeling grateful for what they have and who they have in their lives.

Mary sits there in stunned silence and her face seems to reveal multiple levels of internal conflict. She hears about everything they have that she does not and is forced to realize how she is not a part of their private unions. She somehow tolerates it without breaking down or taking over. I think that is the result of having Gerri as a firm, defined container for her to find form and meaning for her life, even if that form is painful and without much meaning.

In this final scene, Mary is no longer protesting what others have, she is no longer invading others' privacy to take over what she wants, and she is no longer demanding to be the center of attention. Her face seems to portray two aspects of a person's initial depressive position experience. Mary looks shell-shocked and punch-drunk with grief and sadness from finally actually realizing and acknowledging that others have lives separate than hers and that she is truly alone in her own existence. She is literally and figuratively across the table from them. She has to see for once that while she is at the same table, there is a table that separates them.

Mary seems to be feeling the depth of depressive desolation, the moment of realization that her world is barren, lost, and decimated. It is the moment after the bomb hits the city and the citizens look around to see nothing but rumble and that only wreckage remains.

Joan Riviere (1936) has described the depressive position and its unique suffering in detail. She examines the painful road to whole-object functioning and psychological integration as necessary yet almost unbearable at times. She states,

> The depressive position is the situation in which all one's loved ones *within* are dead and destroyed, all goodness is dispersed, lost, in fragments, wasted and scattered to the winds; nothing is left *within* but utter desolation. Love brings sorrow, and sorrow brings guilt; the intolerable tension mounts, there is no escape, one is utterly alone, there is no one to share or help. Love must die because love is dead. Besides, there would be no one to feed one, and no one whom one could feed, and no food in the world. And more, there would still be magic power in the undying persecutors who can never be exterminated – the ghosts.
>
> (Riviere 1936, p. 313)

In the film's final scene, Mary seems to be living within this shocking and terrifying moment that Riviere describes. Mary is in shock and fully engulfed in grief. This is the more mature state of psychic regret (Kavaler-Adler 2004), a genuine feeling of remorse for what one has done to self and other.

As the film ends, the camera comes in close to Mary's face and her expression of sorrow. I believe that there is a small moment in which she seems able to bear this sorrow enough to consider the next stage of the depressive position. Out of depression, sorrow, regret, and remorse comes the hope and desire to rebuild for the first time. Creation, birth, life, redemption, and renewal are possible in this state of fragile hope. Regarding this important moment of psychic development, Riviere (1936, p. 313) states,

> [In the *depressive position*, the patient's] sense of failure, of inability to remedy matters is so great, the belief in better things is so weak: despair is so near. And analysis means unmasking, that is, to the patient, displaying in all its reality, making real, 'realizing', this despair, disbelief and *sense of failure*, which then in its turn simply means death to the patient. It becomes

quite comprehensible why he will have none of it. Yet, with what grains of hope he has, he knows that no one but an analyst ventures to approach even to the fringes of these problems of his; and so he clings to analysis, as a forlorn hope, in which at the same time he really has no faith.

Mary seems, for only a painful moment, to allow others to exist independently and happily while she contemplates finding the shattered pieces of her life and starting to consider what she might do with them. I believe this was all facilitated and encouraged by Gerri finally becoming a different, defined, limiting container who let Mary know she had someone to believe in her but that she now needed to believe in herself as well.

Discussion

In the paranoid-schizoid position, central elements of experience include a prey-versus-predator mentality and a starving infant searching for an idealized nourishing mother but haunted by a demonized, cruel, and neglectful mother. Mary was usually operating as this lost child in a cruel world with her demanding to be rescued, fed, and loved by Gerri. I believe that, as a result of Gerri's new identity as a more active and defining container, Mary was able and willing to approach certain elements of the depressive position. Specifically, she was able to face the reality of others having their own objects they love, face her own failures, and not try to destroy the other's joy as a way to avoid her own sense of grief, loss, and failure. This is a shift away from the death instinct and the driving force of envy and pathological projective identification as her main way of experiencing the world and relating or not relating to others. Again, this shift was brief, perhaps for only minutes, but I think she caught a glimpse of a different world for that passing moment.

In that brief period, I think Mary could tolerate the defeat and loss of the depressive experience. It was not clear if she could contemplate any hope or the phantasy of rebuilding and creative construction of a life separate and apart from her former captives. Yet, I think she allowed herself to consider it for the briefest of moments. Either way, she allowed others their freedom and independence without envious attack.

During most of the film, Mary looks to Gerri, her husband, and son as objects to control, own, and feed from. The manner in which Gerri allows this is useful to consider when exploring the concept of the container and the dynamic of projective identification.

I think there are different levels of containment possible that either help, hinder, or neglect the subject (Waska 2004, 2005). Gerri seems to embody a static, passive container that is like a flimsy bag; it holds Mary but doesn't offer much else. Even worse, Gerri at times seems to be an enabling container, going along with whatever destructive and demanding force Mary brings. This is an unhealthy collaboration between subject and container versus a container object that is able and willing to confront, actively observe (Waska 2012), define, translate, and illuminate the conflicts within the subject and between subject and object. This more limited setting and defining container is what Steiner (1996) speaks of regarding helping the patient towards integration and psychic growth.

Steiner also notes that many patients like Mary want to internalize or kidnap the analyst as their special private container that will always follow them, serve them, and comfort them regardless of what they do. Steiner notes that we as analysts must strive to help the patient internalize a robust, defining, and separate container, the internal experience of the worked through transference.

But, then, we hope to assist the patient in letting go of us as the container and to have them become their own container. This involves a marked transition of grief, loss, and separation that many patients resist (Waska 2002). This is a developmental move Mary clearly has not made but, perhaps with another professional to help, Gerri's support as a friend, and Mary's own motivation to help herself, this could be the eventual reward for her.

Conclusions

This chapter has examined moments in which the film *Another Year*'s main character, Mary, is at the crossroads of realizing and accepting her lost past as well as the positive state of those around her contrasted with her own personal failures and loneliness. These moments of possible tolerance and reflection are all a potential bridge to change, recovery, and growth characteristic of the depressive position. But, in most of the film, this sudden new way of thinking and feeling is overwhelming, and Mary ultimately continues to sink back into envy, self-hatred, despair, and the needy demand on others to give her what she cannot or will not find for herself. All of these dynamics are externally acted out in her drinking problem.

No matter how close Mary gets to tasting a new way of being, she withdraws into her familiar dependent demand, parasitic union, and psychic retreat (Steiner 2011). However, due to Gerri finally confronting Mary and becoming more of a defined and defining container, Mary has a moment of new vision. Suddenly, Gerri is no longer just a flimsy, controlled container with no translating function, a container full of gaping holes in which Mary's love and aggression pass through without comment or understanding. Now, Gerri is a new object for Mary, and Mary seems to respond in a healthy manner, if only for a minute.

In that fleeting space, Mary seems to allow the depressive grief of realizing she is behind in life, on her own, and separate from others. In addition, she suddenly seems to tolerate what others have without envy taking over and compelling her to attack and destroy.

To summarize the dynamics of the depressive position, there are two stages of development. In the first, the subject can tolerate the other as independent and separate. The subject can tolerate, with great pain, the realization of their need for the object and the loss of the object, resulting in the task of finding out how to fend for oneself. Mary was on the verge of this experience. Only in the more mature but difficult to reside within second stage of the depressive position can the subject truly respect, not just tolerate, the success, difference, and separateness of the object. Here, the life instinct takes over and allows for personal freedom, interdependence, and true love of the object as its own entity. The role of the death instinct was strong in Mary's usual relating. She would not usually accept difference or need; she wanted union and gratification of her need without having to acknowledge it or work for it. She killed off separation by her sado-masochistic acting out, making herself the focus of all events.

Tom and Gerri seem to accept those around them without judgment but this seems to be a mix of loving acceptance and neglect. There is a lack of confrontation, request for change, or even asking for an effort towards change. So, is it pure compassion they have for Mary and others or is it also a bit of callous neglect, fear, and turning away from any possible conflict they might encounter if they choose to take a stand on their own behalf or on behalf of Mary? It is not clear whether they are offering a helpful container or simply allowing Mary to languish "as is" without any form of effort, reaction, or demand. Unconditional love from the object is an idealized vision, a myth; but perhaps a myth perpetuated by Gerri, Tom, and Mary as a collective pathological organization.

Mary seemed to desperately need a functioning, defined, and defining container but could not locate one in those around her or in herself. Bion and many others have explored the issues of the container function in psychic growth and found it to be crucial to healthy living. Steiner (1996) has examined the two stages of optimal containment in the psychoanalytic process. Steiner writes about how the subject wants the analyst to be a parental container for them to relieve anxiety but does not want to give up their control over that container relationship. Steiner notes that, eventually, we hope the patient can face the grief, loss, and trauma of not having the analyst provide that containment any longer and in its place the patient becomes their own container, hopefully providing the same sorts of understanding, limits, and forgiveness.

Steiner (1996, p. 1076) states:

> Two stages [of the reversal of projective identification process] seem to be involved, in the first of which the object is used as a container to collect, integrate and give meaning to disparate parts of the self. Bion (1962) suggested that it is through being understood in this way that the projections become more acceptable to the patient, who can take them back in a modified form. In my view, however, containment relieves anxiety and provides a sense of being understood but does not in itself permit a true separateness to be achieved, so that projections are not fully withdrawn until the second stage of mourning is worked through. In the first stage the patient internalizes an object containing parts of the self still inextricably bound to it, and the loss of the object during actual separations is denied by a phantasy of omnipotent possession of it. The relief from anxiety comes from a sense of being understood by the analyst and relies on the analyst's authority.

A simple example of this may be applied to Mary and others who have drug or alcohol problems and go into a treatment program. Initially, if in a recovery program, the person will fear the mandated drug tests and the consequences of being caught "dirty." This fear of being caught will often keep the person sober but it is through the fear of a persecutory parental container that they comply. This is a paranoid-schizoid experience of containment, in which fear of punishment and being made to comply comprises a sadomasochistic me-versus-them mentality. For Mary, we can imagine this would be her initial way of coping if and when she tried to get sober.

Next, the container becomes something much more useful, compassionate, and important to the subject, an object to love and trust. It is still a defining, limiting, and authoritative object but one that the subject believes would love them back. There is dependence without the former slave/master resentment. When an addict or alcoholic has a sponsor in a recovery program they have to answer to them, but it is hopefully a caring and nurturing bond that the subject feels they can depend on and trust. So, rather than persecution and domination, the authority is respected and listened to for learning and support. This is more a move into depressive function as guilt emerges more than a prey and predator or foe mentality. Here, we find many addicts wanting to stay sober because of what the sponsor told them or showed them. If there is temptation of drinking, the subject may fear the disappointment but not the attack and revenge of the sponsor. The subject may feel so guilty about letting the sponsor down that they will not drink. So, these are elements that embody Steiner's first stage of containment.

While this situation is helpful to a recovering alcoholic in the short term, such a long-term dependence would not be so helpful. This is the authoritative container Steiner says must be given up, mourned, and rebuilt in one's mind.

In this regard, Steiner (1996, pp. 1076–1077) states,

> Understanding as opposed to being understood has to arise from within and depends on a capacity to think and judge for oneself, so that it involves a relinquishment of a dependence on the views and judgments of authority figures, including the analyst.
>
> Such a relinquishment ushers in the second phase, which represents a move towards independence and towards facing the pain of the mourning process. If containment has been successful and the patient feels more understood, the object that is internalized is less persecuting and may facilitate movement towards the second phase.
>
> In this phase the reality of dependence on the object has to be acknowledged and then the reality of the loss of the object has to be faced in order for mourning to be worked through, and both are often vehemently resisted. It is clear that projective identification itself obscures the reality of the separateness between self and object, and it is this reality that is re-established if the projections can be returned.

The parallel to Mary or to others in recovery from addiction would be the subject internalizing the sponsor/container function as their own and becoming their own sponsor/container. Here, the subject would have their own desire to stay sober and they would be supportive, understanding, limiting, and, when needed, authoritative to themselves.

This whole cycle is similar to the idea of teaching children not to steal. At first, they don't steal because someone is watching them and would catch them and punish them. Later, they internalize their parents' commands about stealing and don't because they feel guilty about letting their parents down. They want to do the right thing to please their parents. Later, in a more mature manner, they simply decide that stealing is not something they want to do. They believe it is not a good thing. Therefore, they are following their own guidance.

Mary is probably in the first stage of Steiner's containment as the result of Gerri saying no, voicing limits and difference. In the final scene of the film, Mary is close to the pain and mourning of Steiner's second stage of containment but only in a very fragile and temporary manner. She is nowhere near fully integrating it or being able to bear its psychic reality.

The real value of Gerri becoming a useful container for Mary lies in the chance for Mary to reflect upon herself and learn about her way of being so that she can finally have a choice about change and growth. This new self-knowledge is only possible when the mind is not hindered by the blur of pathological projective identification and the disorganizing lack of containment (Joseph 1988; Waska 2010a, 2010b, 2010c, 2011a).

Steiner (1996, p. 1076) states,

> I will argue that the reversibility of projective identification depends on the individual's capacity to face psychic reality and in particular to confront the reality of loss and to go through the mourning process that results from this confrontation. Indeed I believe that it is precisely through the process of mourning that projections are removed from the object and returned to the self.

Mary was reluctant to learn about herself and to face knowing who she had been in life, who she was currently in life, and who she was shaping up to be in the future. Gerri failed her as a container throughout most of the film in that she did not help her learn more about herself. This painful yet useful self-knowledge is the emotional bridge Mary needs to find change, transformation, and self-forgiveness.

Knowledge, knowing, and learning are central components to the Kleinian theory of what makes up the human psyche (Waska 2011b, 2013). Klein placed the desire to know the object alongside the life-and-death instincts as fundamental in understanding human motivation. The subject is curious, envious, and wanting to understand the workings of the object. This creates a desire to be inside the other to taste, test, share, own, and be the other. In healthy development, this involves a thirst for knowledge, a drive to find out, and a talent to solve problems by learning. The unknown becomes something that fuels growth and exploration.

In unhealthy or pathological states, the unknown is unbearable, envy of the other takes over, and a desperate and aggressive attack is launched to find entry into the object and take what is inside. This can result in claustrophobic phantasies, fears of reprisal, revenge, and retribution, as well as a sense of self as inferior and without, that others know and one is clueless and left out. In treatment, many patients display the resistance or fear of knowing themselves, feel trespassed by our wanting to know about them, and rely on a primitive system of withholding or of projecting what is inside out to protect themselves from others knowing more about them.

This was Mary's fate until Gerri offered her a glimpse of hard-to-swallow knowledge about herself and the hard-to-bear idea that hope and change could be possible if she could mourn the old and the current in order to face the unknown future where she could find or build her better self.

Chapter 10

Good Neighbors

A film review lost and without – revenge, capture, and substitution

In summarizing the film *Good Neighbors*, Wikipedia tell us that Louise (Emily Hampshire) works as a waitress in a Chinese restaurant in a neighborhood of Montreal where she lives, and has become obsessed with the story of a recent spate of serial murders committed in her area. She scours the newspapers for stories about each victim. The latest victim is a co-worker who last spoke of a blond, muscular man whom she met at the bar, with whom she had a drink after she got off work at midnight.

Louise's wheelchair-bound downstairs neighbor Spencer (Scott Speedman) shares her predilection up to a point, but mostly likes to keep to himself. Then a young elementary schoolteacher, Victor (Jay Baruchel), moves into the building, having recently returned to the city from a trip in China. The three live on separate floors.

Victor eagerly wants to make friends with Louise and Spencer, who are reluctant to form a friendship with him, as they find him only slightly more agreeable than the drunken, foul-mouthed tenant Valérie (Anne-Marie Cadieux), who hates Louise's cats. As the trio's relationships develop, it becomes apparent that each is a troubled character. Louise's life is focused more on her cats, Mozart and Tia Maria than on humans. Victor is almost a benign stalker, keen to ingratiate himself with the other tenants, especially Louise, upon whom he appears to develop a crush, inventing an imaginary love life; Victor also talks to his mirror. Spencer appears the most well adjusted of the three, despite his handicap. As the walls are paper-thin, it is hard to keep secrets in this apartment complex.

From a psychoanalytic perspective, everyone in this film seems to be trying to take over, substitute, or destroy the other. Each character is a predator and everyone is a potential victim. So, Louise wants the immediate and constant affection of her cats but is put off and irritated when they have their own needs such as going outside for a walk. Her two cats try to get through Spencer's window to eat his fish, but they end up being hunted down and killed by Valérie. Without her cats, Louise is lost and quickly takes over Victor's new cat and uses it for her parasitic-like ownership and immediate gratification. When she learns that Valérie has killed her cats, she uses her fascination and envy of the serial killer to plot revenge. She devises an elaborate plan in which she uses Victor for his sperm to fake a rape of Valérie after she slits her throat.

Louise is someone who has no one and is without the capacity to engage. She merely wants to own a controllable source of love or attention and uses her object, the cats, in a perverse manner to substitute her absent object that she never grieves for, only finding revenge and ownership of a captured soothing object, never a reciprocal love.

Spencer has lost his wife in a car accident and now he pretends to need his wheelchair and seems withdrawn and helpless. But we quickly learn that he enjoys controlling and identifying with his predatory fish to whom he feeds live fish with a smile. He throws something at Louise's cats, not to defend his fish but to attack the cats. He sneaks out at night and kills women, and rapes them afterwards. He seems to need this revenge and savage dominance to avoid any trace of loss or emptiness. He seeks a substitute for his wife and fills himself with power and contempt. When he realizes that Victor may turn him in, he enlists Louise to kill him. When he sees Louise returning from killing Valérie as he is returning from a kill of his own, they treat each other as simple business-people crossing in the street. He uses that information about her to strike a deal to kill Victor off but Louise double-crosses him to protect herself.

Valérie was a woman who was always angry at someone for something. This drove her boyfriend away and she is now a lonely, angry woman reduced to harassing people over the phone and plotting to kill Louise's cats. She fluctuates from angry and demanding with her boyfriend on the phone to desperate and despairing. She was often drunk and raging and then depressed and crying. But it seemed that she did not want to be with her boyfriend but merely needed and demanded somebody to fill her emptiness and loss. She wanted a substitute and felt entitled to it. The world had done her wrong and she wanted revenge.

The manager of this apartment of single, lonely, predatory strangers was a single woman who seemed to do her best to put out the fires and dramas. On the surface she was nice and warm, just as her tenants seemed initially to be. So, she hung decorations at holidays and greeted the tenants when they arrived. But, whenever she had a chance, she was a vicious gossip with the physical therapist who came often to give Spencer a massage and look in on his health. These two women, who seemed to fulfill roles of service and understanding, actually relished in trading their latest barbed criticism and put-downs on each tenant. They both seemed lonely and without, so they took over the goodness of others and projected their own badness. They had contempt, envy, and disgust for everyone.

At first, Victor is portrayed as a nervous, timid and innocent schoolteacher who tries to be nice and friendly to Spencer and Louise. But, very quickly, he develops a secret crush on Louise and tells his friends that they are engaged. When her cats are killed, he brings in a new cat to entice her to him. Louise uses him for his cat and he seems to work around this by making her sleep in his bed to be with the cat. So, he takes her over and uses her as a substitute fiancée.

He ends up telling the police that he has seen Spencer out in the street at night and fears he is the serial killer. He seems to do this to take him away from Louise because those two have a history of talking with each other in a way that is clearly meant as a sort of cigarette break in the day of two completely narcissistic, shut-off, and without-engagement individuals who simply must take over someone or something to substitute what could be a loving exchange with another human being. Instead, all the tenants and the manager seem to live independent lives looking for opportunities to take over others, substituting real human contact with a lifeless vessel that provides gratification.

Revenge, control, dominance, and aggression lie very close to the surface. There is a façade of strangers getting along and conversing, but really this is all a bloody warfare with a cemetery for a battlefield. Endless longing and crippling emptiness define the players who refuse to mourn or share, and instead invade, infuse, and infect to gain their temporary flicker of power, fulfillment, and twisted relating.

Discussion

This movie provides thought-provoking entertainment as well as a chance to reflect upon the powerful underbelly of some narcissistic patients whom we encounter. While never to the violent or sadistic degree of this film, I believe we do encounter individuals who are so intent upon finding someone to prey on for their needs and to use us in order to not face sorrow, envy, or loss that we feel taken over, used, and held to ransom. The obvious type of patient that fits this bill is the more paranoid-schizoid type of borderline individual. Here, we have someone who is more like the character Victor or Valérie who is desperate to have someone to hook into, anchor into, and attach to in a predatory or parasitic way. Then, they feel claustrophobic, taken over, or invaded through projective identification, and flee or push the analyst out of their lives with a vengeance. As a result, they feel abandoned, lonely, and resentful and begin the cycle all over again.

Some more narcissistic patients are better built psychologically to avoid this breakdown but they are still empty, desperate, and fragile. They don't show their desperation and pleading, but instead seek revenge and focus their rage and entitlement on the analyst, and in the counter-transference we feel like a spittoon or Kleenex that is used and discarded without any remorse.

Finally, there are patients operating in a primitive depressive mode, trying to avoid grief and mourning by constantly substituting their fallen objects with the next best thing. Here, we have a transference in which the analyst is forced to be a certain type of object and, no matter what we say or do, the patient hears us as the familiar, desired, or designated object they demand.

But, no matter what degree of internal chaos, anxiety, or rage exists, these are all individuals who are without. Their inner worlds are without any stable, soothing object that they can trust and attach to. Due to various unconscious conflicts and the excessive use of projective identification, these individuals ignore or discard the objects they do or could have, and instead find a substitute that they can control, shape, and use for their immediate and rigidly defined gratification. We become what they want and lose who we are as they continue to feel empty, taking in only what they imagine will fulfill their exact demands and what will makes us into their desired or dreaded object. We end up like Frankenstein, a creature created by and for the crazy professor who all alone in his lab tries to piece together something from multiple tragedy and incurable loss.

Part V

Problems with psychic equilibrium

Chapter 11

Does the patient desire psychic growth or restoration of psychic equilibrium?

The life-and-death instincts in the counter-transference

Patients who operate on the edge of the depressive position (Klein 1935, 1940) with a fragmented, primitive, or disorganized experience of whole-object functioning can be as challenging to reach in the analytic situation as the more primitive paranoid-schizoid patient (Klein 1946). Establishment and maintenance of analytic contact with either type of patient is precarious at best (Waska 2007, 2012) when the individual is struggling to keep their internal status quo rather than risk change (Waska 2005, 2006).

The patient's quest to maintain their existing psychic equilibrium (Feldman 2004; Hargreaves and Varchenker 2004) and its destructive or pathological defensive organization (Steiner 1987) creates a mindset in which the patient consciously wants change and insight but unconsciously experiences our efforts to help them change as threatening to themselves and to their objects (Joseph 1983). There is a death instinct-based reliance on bad, unavailable, or fragile objects through excessive use of projective identification. One result of this is that the patient's mind is left empty and barren, creating a devastating state of emptiness and despair. Or, the constant and intense projective mechanisms are so rigid that they create unbending loyalty to very select, narrow, and one-dimensional images of self and other that must be replayed over and over again without deviation (Waska 2004).

Typically, patients enter treatment when their psychic equilibrium is out of balance and they are facing sudden increased levels of depressive anxiety or paranoid dread. Often it is a bit of both, as some of these patients exist in an emotional no-man's land. Instead of finding pathological safety from both positions in a psychic retreat (Steiner 1993, 2011), they end up feeling incredibly exposed to the more primitive aspects of both positions without any psychological shelter. In this psychic foxhole (Waska 2010a), they feel as if they, and often their objects, are without a protective skin, raw and exposed to any and all elements.

In treatment, it is common for such patients to try to re-establish their former pathological organization (Rosenfeld 1987; Steiner 1990), to find a psychic retreat, or to regress to some other, more primitive manner of finding respite from their emotional demons. Initially, they may engage the analyst and establish a level of analytic contact (Waska 2010b), but, at some point, they become alarmed at the unknown future and their now shifting internal world, which we see as positive growth. They react defensively to this shift towards life and individuation. At that point, they often abruptly terminate treatment or begin a pattern of acting out that greatly endangers the treatment process. They try to find their former link to pathological, ancient, and archaic object-relational patterns and see our invitation for change as odd, useless, or dangerous. We are suddenly the authoritative, greedy, and out-of-touch object that has stopped supporting them and is trying to force them or their objects into being something unknown and unwanted, something they feel to be either overly constricted or dangerously out of control.

Perelbberg (2009) notes that the hard-to-reach borderline patient is always challenging the analytic setting, and creates a jarring impact upon the analyst in the counter-transference. The analyst often feels excluded and/or expelled from the patient's internal world. These more primitive patients close down the opportunities that psychoanalytic treatment offers, relying on the more confined and defended aspects of the death instinct and the repetition compulsion. As a result of this drastic splitting process, if the analyst does not join the patient in their lifeless state, the analyst is placed in the service of the life instinct, making any and all efforts to create emotional links to curiosity, change, or growth.

Sodre (2004) notes that when such excessive projective identification is employed there can be a marked inner confusion and a loss of any real sense of self. I think this is especially the case for the more borderline or psychotic patient existing in the paranoid-schizoid realm (Waska 2010c, 2010d). The other condition that occurs (Sodre 2004) more often with troubled depressive patients is a marked rigidity of character, in which exaggerated, artificial, or one-dimensional roles are religiously adhered to. The self and the object are enlisted into very specific and unforgiving roles, and the patient strongly defends these roles to avoid, not emptiness or internal chaos but the return of the opposite state of mind.

These are patients who operate on the primitive edge of depressive phantasies in which they suffer with very fragile phantasies of loss, control, and difference. They must manage and control the object at all costs. They suffer with persecutory guilt (Grinberg 1964) and an avoidance of personal need so as to not experience the great conflict of greed, abandonment, and loss they fear at all times. These fears are noted by Feldman (1997) when he describes how patients use projective identification to minimize the differences between their ancient, core object-relational bonds and the new, different, and unknown relationship which the analyst represents.

When this occurs, the transference and the motive of the projective identification have to do with the defensive workings of the death instinct in which the sources of need, difference, knowledge, and separation are attacked or voided (Segal 1993). In these clinical moments, the analyst is placed in the service of the life instinct and pushed to speak up on behalf of change, growth, and difference. Otherwise, the analyst may find himself pulled into the other direction, to end up on the side of the death instinct, feeling hopeless, useless, and lost. This is where the analyst begins to give up or simply coast in a neutral fashion as the treatment slowly fails and fades away (Feldman 1994; Steiner 2000).

With regard to the death instinct as it unfolds in the clinical situation, Feldman (2000) notes how the death instinct is seen operating in how some patients will try to attack, distort, or deny the meaning and value of the analyst's mind, the analyst's interpretations, or the progress established thus far. They do this in order to spoil and devalue the threatening new and unknown, rendering all to the same and any new back to the old. They take the life out of the relationship and the life out of the evolving analytic process so as to bring back their psychic equilibrium and the known aspects of their archaic object-relational functioning. Their gratification comes from spoiling and undermining the opportunity for any new, different, unknown, or uncontrolled aspects of self or object to emerge. The only thing that is permitted to exist is what was and what is, not anything that could be.

So, as a result of these patients' reliance upon the death instinct and destructive forms of projective identification, there are confusing counter-transference moments. In these moments the analyst ends up numb, listless, and hopeless. One is pulled towards a sense of apathy and resignation (Feldman 2009; Waska 2011a). Or, in defensive reaction, there may be a manic attempt to urge the patient to change, trying to keep them motivated as part of a desperate depressive desire to keep them and the relationship alive (Steiner 2006; Waska 2011b). The analyst may end up trying to rally the patient or convince them to not quit treatment or to not give up emotionally. When blamed, devalued, and attacked, the analyst may end up trying to prove their worth, coming close to almost apologizing and begging the patient to stay as part of a sadomasochistic enactment.

Case material

Albert and Bonnie were a borderline couple whom I saw for six months. Over that period of time I helped them explore the meaning behind the incredible chaos that shaped their relationship. They had been fighting and yelling at each other for months with threats of a breakup becoming the norm. They both had a lifestyle of random sex with others and, while they agreed in principle on this "open relationship," they both felt hurt, betrayed, and cheated by this arrangement and it led to many fights. They also drank a great deal and used many different drugs, which only seemed to heighten both of their sensitivities to feeling slighted, used, or forgotten.

Albert had supported Bonnie financially for most of the five years they had been together. Emotionally, he seemed to experience this as a way of rescuing his broken and weak object as well as having constant control over it. So, Albert ended up not only anxious and concerned but resentful and judgmental. He reminded Bonnie to take her medications for depression, made her doctor appointments for her, and recommended who to call for job interviews. Then, in a passive-aggressive manner, Albert would label her efforts as either worthy or not worthy. This left Bonnie feeling inferior and enraged. She would often spend most of the session screaming at Albert for his "shitty, arrogant treatment" of her, leaving Albert intimidated and dominated by her angry presence.

Then, Bonnie would use Albert as an object that she could lash out against, waving herself about as a weak victim whom Albert never understood or supported emotionally. She demanded to be respected for whatever efforts she did make, even when they were obviously destructive or counterproductive. She lashed out at Albert for being "fat and lazy," and threatened to leave him if he didn't become more interesting and attractive.

In response, Albert would break down in a fit of hysterical guilt, crying and telling me how he was the one ruining the relationship. Since this guilt and self-blame hid Albert's more resentful and angry feelings towards Bonnie's way of using him and not really making much of an effort to be an equal partner, I interpreted that Albert left me to voice his negative feelings towards Bonnie. He could look innocent while I expressed his desire to set limits and be respected. This was a projective identification defense in which Albert was filling me up with his most feared feelings, leaving him safe and out of the picture and me to do his dirty work. This was part of the total transference (Joseph 1985) which created particular hardships in the complete counter-transference (Waska 2011a, 2011b).

Bonnie would switch wildly between feeling crippled with suicidal depression to trying to convince me and Albert that she was happy, stable, on the verge of great changes, and not needing any help from Albert or from analytic treatment. Then, she would collapse and feel overwhelmed and useless. After months of boasting proudly of how independent she was and how she never needed to rely on Albert for anything, Bonnie's borderline neediness and emptiness broke through. When Albert was out of town for a work trip and we did not meet for our usual session, Bonnie had a panic attack and was hospitalized. Albert had to fly back to take care of her. Bonnie told me she didn't realize how much she needed Albert and how much their closeness meant to her until this incident. There was a great deal of important reflection and meaningful discussion about the relationship during that session.

When they came in for their next session, Albert and Bonnie announced that they would only be coming in every two weeks from now on "because we are now doing so well." In the counter-transference I wanted to shout out, "What? Wait a minute! You are definitely not ready to cut back. In fact, —." This transference/counter-transference situation is quite common with such disorganized and out-of-reach patients. They are experiencing psychological fragmentation and want relief from pain and anxiety but don't want to face the unknown of difference and change and the threat of loss or betrayal (Waska 2002). So, there is a constant and confusing pull and push in the transference. They had a moment of healthy reflection and temporary integration, a shift from their normal acting out; but now they seemed to use this as a springboard to deny their mutually fragile state of mind and their need for further treatment. They appeared to be reconstituting their pathological organization around which they had structured their relationship from the beginning.

As a result, in the counter-transference, the analyst feels as if they are in a washing machine, churned back and forth. With this clinical situation it is easy to act out in reaction to such back-and-forth emotional shoving. Trying to contain my jarred feelings, I asked Albert and Bonnie about their idea of cutting back. They said things had improved a great deal so they were thinking of either stopping or coming less often. Albert cited how busy he was trying to lose weight and attending his own personal therapy. Bonnie said she felt things were going smoothly now and she was busy looking for a job.

In response I felt devalued. I felt much less important than Albert's weight-loss program and I was put off by this miraculous cure they were both celebrating. So I acted out by saying,

> You are saying things are going so well. I am glad you feel that way and I agree we are making progress. But it was just two weeks ago that Bonnie was in the hospital. I think we have some things to keep working on and we need to meet regularly to do that.

While what I said was probably correct and necessary, I was saying it as the result of my feeling thrown away.

When Albert repeated that he didn't want to come in so often, I again felt put in the position of being the one who suddenly had to stand up for life, for optimal treatment frequency, and for the severity of their separate and mutual illness. I said, "I don't think I can help you seeing you less and you would not get what you want out of it. So, I cannot do that." In other words, I set a limit as an advocate of life and growth, but it also felt as if I was giving them an ultimatum and acting out my anger.

I think Albert and Bonnie provide an example of how certain patients come to us for psychic relief and rebalancing but are unconsciously avoiding and working against a more whole-object transformation and against any shift into psychic change or psychological growth. They are reluctant to face the unknown challenges and rewards of the depressive position and do their best to remain in the familiar shell of their pathological defenses and pathological organization (Rosenfeld 1987).

Through our time together, working analytically, I think Albert and Bonnie found themselves on the verge of a new way of relating, thinking, and feeling. This created a threat to their regular psychic equilibrium, so they decided to circle the wagons around what they knew and how they had been. I was now the threat. I was the bearer of uncertainty, of pain, loss, and guilt as well as a brand new way for them to be with each other that felt dangerous and different. Thus, their death-instinct defenses came to bear and I had to be the threatening voice of life.

Regarding the depressive position, the importance of trying to reach this developmental experience, and the anxiety associated with this transition, Steiner (1992, p. 53) notes that the individual has to face his inability to protect the object. Suddenly,

> his psychic reality includes the realization of the internal disaster created by his sadism and the awareness that his love and reparative wishes are insufficient to preserve his object which must be allowed to die with the consequent desolation, despair, and guilt.

In this regard, in order to move towards the depressive position and its valuable psychological elements of more mature and stable ego functioning, Albert would have to realize that he could no longer, in phantasy, control and rescue Bonnie. He would have to face and own his own anger and judgment as well as the way it affected Bonnie. Albert would have to let Bonnie be herself even if that meant she was depressed and unable to be the person he wanted her to be. And, as a result, Albert might realize he was angry with Bonnie or might feel he didn't want to be with her at all. Then, he would have to face the damage to and loss of his object.

So, Albert was struggling with difficult aspects of the depressive position but in a primitive manner indicated by his more manic reaction to these relational risks and conflicts. The more primitive edge of the depressive position involves splitting and desperate manic retreats into denial and magical reparation (Feldman 1992; Steiner 1979). The patient suffers a split between seeking to save and control a weak, dependent object that is never able to mature, and the rage and disappointment of not being rewarded, served, and obeyed by this object, even though they feel they have sacrificed so much and paid so much attention to it.

This primitive depressive splitting protects the ego from the ultimate loss and pain of having to let go of the object. The patient doesn't have to realize that they have their own needs that may in fact create pain to the object or conflict between the two of them. Albert seemed to be immersed in this type of internal struggle and psychological stand-off for much of the time.

For Bonnie, she seemed to struggle more with paranoid-schizoid anxieties of loss (Waska 2002) as well as volatile fluctuating views of herself and others as strong, superior, and independent, or weak, needy, and failing. In fearing the loss of the object, she was much more afraid of how that loss would affect her than worrying about the fate of the object. This was in contrast to Albert who was in fear of loss as it might result in Bonnie's demise.

While it is extremely common for the more difficult patient to not maintain any sort of consistent, predictable, grounded, or ongoing stable relationship with the analyst, it is nevertheless vexing and challenging to deal with. These more turbulent patients often make rather sudden and jolting announcements of their departure, their disappointment, or their lack of involvement. Suddenly they don't care, and blame you for not giving them enough. Or, they say they have found the happiness they were looking for when it seems obvious they are still struggling with rather severe states of paranoid-schizoid anxiety or debilitating depressive conflicts regarding love, hate, and knowledge.

In fact, it is not uncommon for these types of patients to merely leave a phone message indicating they will not ever be returning. In addition, there is neither explanation for the premature termination nor any mention of the money they still owe. Or, in some cases, there is not even a message. They simply stop showing up and never return our calls. All this constitutes behaviors, attitudes, and ways of relating that easily bring out some sort of acting out in the analyst. We can feel in many different ways, but I think the two primary reactions tend to be the over-activation of the life-and-death instincts in the counter-transference as a result of the aggressive use of projective identification in the transference.

Because these chaotic and brittle patients are so caught up in this intense storm of life-and-death instinct conflicts that are intensified by their paranoid-schizoid or primitive depressive phantasies, we end up feeling a combination of these extreme affects through their projective identification efforts. In the counter-transference we alternate and ricochet between them, but usually one becomes our primary method of coping. In the midst of the patient's withdrawal, resistance, and race to reconstitute their former pathological defensive system instead of risking a new way of being, we find ourselves swept up in the deep waters of either the life or death instincts.

As mentioned before, these two counter-transference experiences crystalize in the analyst either giving in and giving up or taking up the challenge of revitalizing the patient. We either lose our motivation or we try to force motivation back into the patient. We sign up to the funeral of the analytic relationship or we try to perform heroic life resuscitation on it.

Case material continued

All these feelings were certainly a challenge for me in Albert and Bonnie's case. In the next session, their individual ways of relating to me and to each other crystalized. They both looked rather preoccupied when they sat down so I asked them about it. Albert told me they had been thinking about stopping the treatment for reasons of time and money but mostly because they had been "doing so well, communicating really good, and getting along very smoothly." Reflecting on the struggles I felt in the last session and realizing I was once again being drawn into a projective identification dynamic, I noted how I now served change, growth, and difference, but in a way that made them see me as advocating conflict, tension, and uncertainty. In the last session, they had reacted to that by suddenly professing harmony, smoothness, and peace. I had become the one now disrupting their desire for familiar fusion and former safe states of psychic equilibrium.

So, I tried to proceed with caution, realizing that no matter what I did, short of giving up by allowing my analytic commitment and identity to waver, wither, and die, I would be interrupting their psychic equilibrium. In addition, in that moment, I think I was being filled with the awful feelings of resentment, concern, and disagreement that Albert felt towards Bonnie, but he felt it was too dangerous to own them. So, he had to get rid of them or Bonnie would be hurt and become enraged. It was easier and safer to jettison them into me through his silence.

This is the type of depressive position reaction that may occur when the patient feels in danger of damaging, triggering, or displeasing their object. They will do whatever it takes to control the object, save the object, and stop the object being displeased by them, even if it means killing off their own feelings and opinions to maintain the psychic equilibrium of the pathological organization that exists between them. They hang onto that which holds them together even if it is also what pulls them apart. It is all about control and manipulation in the service of keeping the object happy, present, and available, but it also creates a great deal of animosity and selfishness in the subject. They try to seem selfless on the outside but they feel wanting, waiting, and hungry on the inside. So, I think Albert was projecting some of these toxic struggles into me at this point in the session.

I said, "There seem to be a few issues still going on that we are making progress with but still could be improved." Albert said he felt they were "stretched pretty thin" with time and money and "the need to just be and relax from our busy schedules."

Suddenly, Bonnie yelled, "Why in the world would we want to ever come back here after the crap you said last time?" I asked for details and noted her sudden switch to this aggressive attack mode. She said,

> You heard me talk about all the success I have had in turning things around, how I decided last week to start looking for a job. That is huge! I actually started looking at my resumé and thinking of where I want to start sending it. Did you support me and tell me I was doing well? Fuck NO! You started to drag me down and tell me I wasn't ever going to find a job. You had to bring up what I would do if I didn't find a job in six months and would be out of money. How dare you! This is fucking crap! I can't picture ever coming back here. We came in last time feeling positive and you made a point of bringing us down!

I felt attacked and noted to myself that Bonnie was now yelling at me with the exact same accusation she hurled at Albert a few months back when Albert asked her what she was going to do if she didn't find a job soon. I said,

> You are seeing me as a bad person right now who is against you. But what I did say and what I do think is that you are trying to turn things around. It is important that you decided to find a conventional job. In addition, I wanted to hear the rest of your plan. Hopefully you will get what you want. But, if you don't, I am curious about your backup plan.

Bonnie continued to yell at me and accuse me of "only being cruel and negative." Probably in a position of defensive enactment I said, "I am simply echoing what Albert said a while ago." I noticed myself saying that and felt I was now deflecting Bonnie's attack. I continued,

> There have been several times since I have known you that you suddenly felt better and confident and talked about working hard to find a job. You were very confident it would happen but then it did not and Albert was very anxious since he is paying all the bills. You got very defensive when he asked you about a backup plan, just as you are now angry with me for that. We see you trying but also want to support you even if this plan doesn't work out. We want to help you find an answer in some form no matter how long it takes.

So, I think my interpretations were correct and helpful, but they also emerged from this place of defensive enactment.

At this point Albert said he was very happy to see Bonnie trying so hard and was very supportive, but he "would feel anxious and worried until the day you get the job. And, I do want to know that if you have to, you will just get a job regardless of what it is. I need to know that to feel okay."

I said to Albert,

> That is one of the first times you have spoken up for your own needs. Most of the time, you have been trying to manage, save, rescue, and control Bonnie and in the process you sacrifice yourself and then feel resentful. But, now you are saying something about your caring for both Bonnie and for yourself.

Here, I was interpreting Albert's sudden shift into more mature depressive functioning in which he could let go of his control over his object and protect himself, even if that meant losing sight of his object. In addition, he was risking hurting his object by stating his own needs; but, by doing so, Albert was also strengthening the relationship by promoting two strong, independent objects that were still close and loving.

The combination of my making those interpretations, my not acting out in any ongoing defensive manner, and Albert standing up for himself all seemed to contain and calm Bonnie down, leaving her feeling a little more secure and less aggressive. Bonnie said she was "aware of my responsibilities to the relationship. I am working hard to keep them up." This sounded like a more mature moment in which she was less in the grip of paranoid-schizoid anxieties and could see her objects with less distortion and a little more reality.

We decided, at my urging, to meet again the following week and carry on the discussion about whether or not they would continue treatment. Not coming as any surprise, I received an email message from Albert a few days later. It read:

I wanted to drop you a quick line and let you know that we will be canceling our therapy sessions from now on. We have decided at this time to end our professional relationship with you. We thank you for your help during a critical time in our relationship and owe you our gratitude for helping us weather the worst of the storm. After discussing it at length, we feel we'll be better served by taking a break from therapy. We will be looking for a new therapist in the New Year.

Regards, Albert and Bonnie

Here, I think the transference profile continued in the email message. My sense was that Albert was trying to not hurt me by being polite and kind. On a conscious level, I think they were grateful for my help and that I did help them "weather the worst" of a critical time. But, at the end of the message, I think Albert's camouflaged anger and sense of superiority along with Bonnie's devaluing attacks emerged in their being "better served by taking a break" and the more direct blow of "looking for a new therapist in the New Year." I again had to manage my same counter-transference sensation of feeling both a failure and of wanting to somehow manically rise above it all. What is much harder is to have to just be with it "as is" and try to keep learning instead of reacting.

Discussion

The patients being considered in this chapter rely on projective identification as a way to maintain certain rigid and archaic object-relational patterns and defensive organizations. Some of these individuals are borderline and narcissistic, mired in the realm of paranoid phantasies and conflicts. Others exhibit a pre-depressive, primitive foothold into more whole-object functioning while still needing to use splitting and manic control to avoid internal fragmentation and severe states of psychic loss and emotional collapse.

In discussing Betty Joseph's unique approach to working with such difficult patients, Feldman and Spillius (1992) describe how Joseph puts an emphasis on the patient's need to maintain his psychic equilibrium.

They note how Joseph studies the patient's defense against persecutory and depressive anxiety and how, in spite of their conscious wish to change, the patient mobilizes their defenses in order to maintain their existing state of equilibrium. Joseph describes these patients as defensively destructive to self and object as well as being dominated by the death instinct. This was certainly the case with Albert and Bonnie. As a result of their push for this status quo and a withdrawal from learning or change unless it was a change that helped re-establish a psychic equilibrium, they related like the patients Joseph wrote about. Describing this phenomenon, Feldman and Spillius (1992) state:

a patient may for a time behave as if he has lost his capacity for thinking, understanding, or desiring anything, all of which then become the problems of his analyst; by this means such a patient protects himself from the pain and anxiety which would result if he were to accept responsibility for these mental functions himself.

This is what I encountered with Albert and Bonnie, who left me to struggle with life, meaning, and motivation as they slipped back into the security of sameness.

Feldman and Spillius (1992) continue:

> Joseph believes that if the analyst fails to recognize this state of affairs he will be likely to make interpretations which may sound "correct", may even be correct, but which will be ineffective because the crucial transference/ countertransference issue is the patient's projection of thinking capacity into the analyst.

This occurred during my periods of acting out in response to Albert and Bonnie saying they felt great and were ready to end treatment.

Feldman and Spillius (1992) continue:

> Whereas it would be easier to fit in with the patient's defenses, to give up, or to condemn the patient as unsuitable for analysis, Joseph has made this type of difficulty her special focus of interest and research.

As discussed above, I frequently faced these feelings of apathy and resignation before stepping back into the analytic process.

Finally, Feldman and Spillius (1992) note that Joseph "found that patients who failed to improve in analysis were more than usually insistent on maintaining their psychic equilibrium" (p. 3). I think this was the situation in my clinical report. I was able to sustain Albert and Bonnie at the edge of difference and change before they radically retreated to their familiar sameness. In that process, I think there was a degree of internal change with some insight found and internalized but opportunities for deeper and more permanent change were lost.

So, I believe that the analytic process can be a little more hopeful or promising with these hard-to-reach patients than Joseph states; but, in the end, it is a very complicated and overwhelming process (Anderson 1999). With patients working so intensely to maintain their psychic equilibrium, the analytic process is very difficult to keep alive without succumbing to the urge to force it onto life support. It is also very difficult to accept the relational loss with these hard-to-reach patients without wanting to slam the door shut in grim defeat.

We have to bear the experience of only being partially helpful or only helpful for a fleeting moment or phase in their life. We have to tolerate being used to patch a terrible leak in the psychic dam which the patient has learned to live behind. We have to say goodbye and hope that if they want more sometime in the future we have left them with the impression that it is possible, rewarding, and survivable.

Chapter 12

Starving for scraps

The technical challenges of pre-depressive patients desperate to maintain psychic equilibrium

We encounter certain patients in psychoanalytic practice who want help but they define or demand that help in a very particular way. They want us to help them alleviate certain symptoms, stop their current crisis, or save them from impending emotional collapse. All these situations are genuine and the patient feels great anxiety. However, when we are successful in lightening their load and proceed to invite them to be curious about the rest of their life, to expand their perceptions of self and other, to consider the destructive patterns they rely on in their relationships, and to ponder how to enrich their lives going forward, these patients are confused, resistant, and resentful. They feel as though we are not respecting their wishes, not paying attention to their needs, taking over, and blaming them for not pursuing our agenda.

This type of patient comes in with a crisis that seems to be the result of deeper psychological issues; but, once the patient feels better and the crisis passes, they tell us they are done. They came in for help with that crisis and not for anything else. Then they leave, shaking their head in confusion, outrage, or insult at our wanting more than they asked for. They have enlisted us in their quest to restore their psychic equilibrium (Hargreaves and Varchenker 2004; Joseph 1989) so that they can return to their former, familiar object-relational state. They feel threatened when we question that state.

These patients are usually borderline (Grinberg 1977) with a variety of dependent, masochistic, or narcissistic features. They want and they don't want, they plead for attention but then ignore the help that is provided by giving up on themselves and others. They seem to cry out for someone to protect them and soothe them but easily shift to feeling independent and able to care for themselves. These vacillating and volatile aspects of their unconscious object-relational conflicts flood the transference and often leave the analyst spinning or sinking in the counter-transference.

Some of these patients are also struggling at the jagged edge of depressive position functioning; but they experience only the lack of control, persecutory guilt (Grinberg 1964), and extreme loss (Espasa 2002) of that psychic state without the rewards of stability, trust, acceptance, and forgiveness (Hinshelwood 1989) that can be so healing, empowering, and gratifying. To this end, Steiner

(1992, p. 53) describes the essential anxieties of the depressive position when he states:

> [T]he depressive position can thus also be seen to contain gradations within it, particularly in relation to the question of whether loss is feared and denied or whether it is acknowledged and mourning is worked through. I have used this distinction to divide the depressive position into a phase of denial of loss of the object and a phase of experience of the loss of the object.

The patients I am highlighting in this chapter are either more paranoid and borderline or they are these depressive patients who fear loss, deny loss, and retaliate against the threat of loss.

Case material

E came to me in a depressed and anxious state and said, "I am unable to cope and need help in making my way through this weird shitty thing they call life." She told me she hated people and felt the world was an ugly place full of strange people with strange ideas. There was an odd and theatrical manner in how E acted with me. Every movement and every statement was made in an exaggerated, dramatic, and often grotesque form. She twisted her face into a horrible grimace as she spoke haltingly, and twisted her body into hunched, off-balance positions and postures. E told me,

> I saw these strange alien beings called citizens walking towards me on the sidewalk and I felt forced to conform to their bizarre ways of making polite eye contact when in fact I felt on the verge of vomiting on their faces and screaming at the top of my lungs to find some degree of sanity in this lopsided farce we call life!

Her theater of the absurd performance for me was made all the more offputting by her brightly colored Mohawk haircut and huge colorful feathers she used as earrings.

E said she was always the "oddball" growing up and refused to "play the game. I was never part of all the mainstream clichés in school." She said she dressed "as she pleased" and said whatever she thought, which "got me into trouble and made me the target for lots of laughter and ridicule. But, I didn't care. I didn't really care about much of anything. But, then things got really strange." This was her reference to the awful trauma that happened in her final year of high school.

E told me about her adolescence in which she dealt with parents who were often fighting. There was also an ongoing conflict with a mentally disturbed cousin. He became more and more volatile, violent, and unstable. This culminated in E witnessing him murdering her parents four years before I met her.

Given E's state of mind and the degree of trauma and anxiety she was suffering, I offered to meet with her several times each week, but E felt she only wanted to meet with me once a week. She said this in a controlled, neutral manner. I realized she might need to modulate her degree of closeness given her devastating loss, not wanting to risk any similar sense of disconnection. Nevertheless, the way E went about it felt very callous, mechanical, and without an entry point for discussion, exploration, or negotiation.

In the transference, E seemed to want something from me but would not allow anything to emerge from herself in return. When her credit card didn't work and I had to call her, E did not return my calls. When E missed her session without leaving a message, she also didn't return my calls. When I brought it up in the next session since E didn't say a thing about it, she immediately dismissed it as no big deal and said she "had just gotten busy." She did not seem to care about her impact upon me. When I brought up that it could have some helpful meaning to understand this way of relating, E said she "didn't think so" and it "was just the way I operate. I don't usually have any connections or consistent relationships with people so this is going pretty good so far. Consider yourself lucky!" Along with feeling as though I had been given ample warning for what might be ahead, it seemed as if E was asking me to go along with this uncertainty, dismissiveness, and mystery without being able to ever learn about it, ask about it, or know about it. It also seemed as if I was to give to her and she did not seem to want to give back.

In order to not take these states of mind personally and to avoid an enactment process, I reminded myself repeatedly that she was probably giving me a taste of her own trauma, that she was naturally being withholding and self-protective to avoid more pain, and that she was projecting her sense of abandonment and distance into me. I think all these ideas were true and helpful. However, there seemed to be more to it. I think there is a way in which certain damaged patients do not want to consider the opportunity to grow or change because it feels too dangerous (Waska 2005, 2006) and would expose them to the pre-depressive horrors of overwhelming loss and separation (Waska 2002, 2007).

With E, I think this was an extremely intense threat. Therefore, patients like E remain safely barricaded within the ruins of their paranoid-schizoid fortress, clinging to a list of demands or trying to maintain control over all of their objects and reacting strongly if they feel that control is being questioned. The status quo and their psychic equilibrium are critical to constantly rebuild, maintain, and to always stand guard over. The difficult clinical issue is that other patients who suffer from trauma also try to avoid more disappointment, hurt, or loss; but they do profit and respond to the analyst's grounded patience, deliberate empathy, and ever-present encouragement to be more active and free. However, the patients highlighted in this chapter do not seem to budge when we extend our offer of analytic caring and understanding.

Paniagua (2003) has discussed the complex problems that arise when patients strive to establish the transference state of a passive patient being cared for and cured by a knowledgeable, omnipotent doctor/parent. This is one of the transference profiles we encounter with patients who elect to control the analytic situation with passive demand and sadomasochistic manipulation. They are lost in their own state of despair and hopelessness but also use that as a weapon to reel the analyst into joining them in a repetition of specific unconscious phantasies regarding self and other. Some of these phantasies are focused on idealized visions of being rescued and saved, while others focus on the endless despair, lack of control, and powerlessness they feel in relationship to themselves and the world at large.

These two primary transference states naturally evoke parallel countertransference states of rescuing and saving or giving up and feeling like a weak failure. This is the pathological dynamic of the life-and-death instincts activated through excessive reliance on projective identification mechanisms. This intense division of the two psychic states is characteristic of pre-depressive mental perspectives in which the danger of loss and uncertainty is most acute prior to the relief and resolve of depressive integration.

One version of the analyst giving up in the counter-transference is when we end up coasting along forever in a haze of futility and hopelessness. We feel there is not much we can ever do to effect change, so we simply accept the constant state of nothingness, decay, or ongoing emotional disaster. This is an analyst-centered impasse, a counter-transference enactment of numbing resignation.

This state of negative conviction is an acting out of the patient's projection of a defeated container, a failed container, or a hopeless and powerless container. We end up drifting along in the stagnant and crisis-laden waters of the patient's phantasies that constitute their masochistic depression. At times, in this form of counter-transference, we may notice ourselves becoming angry with the patient, wanting to insist that they try to make what seem to be easy and obvious changes. But, for the most part, we notice ourselves going along within a void of any real meaning or hint of life.

If we can rise above this counter-transference morass, we may notice that these patients are reluctant to give up the security of never having to face difference, need, and separation (Segal 1989, 1991; Steiner 2008). In other words, the death instinct crushes the chance to grow and learn (Feldman 2000). And then, the grief of the depressive position is successfully avoided and denied.

One significant counter-transference clue to the patient's deeper unconscious conflicts between love, hate, and learning is when the analyst feels themselves falling into a "you can, you should, and you must" style of relating matched by the patient's "I can't, I don't know how, and I won't" response. Stubborn, unyielding, and unresolvable tones shape the analytic situation. The analyst usually ends up in a state of resentment, resignation, and futility as the end result of this projective identification system in which the very essence of the patient's woes is deposited within the analyst.

The road to finding some success with these patients is to realize that they unconsciously believe that their most important objects are only conditional, fragile, volatile, and easily lost. Not much can be asked of their objects without risking conflict or rejection. A desperate neediness is denied by ignoring the pathological sense of separation, emptiness, and distance so common in their internal relationships which are often played out externally. In addition, feeling in control by taking everything on and never asking for help or by feeling as though there is no one who can help is just as effective in fending off their emotional hunger as the more usual and blatant parasitic nature of their helplessness and their unconscious desire or demand to be guided, parented, and held by others. Thus, we see control, demand, and entitlement alternating with themes of panic, apathy, and a complete lack of autonomy. Or, in some cases, we witness a reactionary super-autonomy or manic independence.

In the transference, there is often a combination of loyal closeness and neediness with neutralized distance. There is a thin and easily broken attachment with the patient seeming to not care when that minimal connection is lost. There is also a lack of any reciprocal flavor to the relationship. The need to be told what to do and pushing for the analyst to take on their most intense and disturbing feelings is in parallel with the patient not having to take action, change, or face the risk of losing their disappointing or abusive, yet familiar and perversely gratifying, object.

Indeed, these patients seem addicted to the pathological relationships they have and the destructive lifestyles they feel trapped in, intellectually acknowledging the negative side of it, but unwilling to experience the emotional strain of saying goodbye to their damaging psychic reality and facing an uncertain future. The analyst represents the frightening opportunity to build a new reality with newer objects and a different vision of self.

In this sense, the depressive position is considered too much to face. In psychoanalytic treatment, we must help these patients give up the security of the old and walk into the new, a place without known guarantee or familiar possession. It is a place of having nothing, a terrifying paranoid-schizoid phantasy but also a chance to create something new. This is a depressive opportunity, a creative possibility.

So, even for those patients with a fragile foothold in a primitive pre-depressive state, they easily retreat to the more basic security of paranoid-schizoid thinking and relating when faced with the prospect of unknown differences, separation, and change.

Patients who exhibit this form of transference and phantasy conflict have often suffered external and internal trauma in childhood. In adulthood, they seem to have little or no faith in themselves or the ability to trust and depend on others in a healthy, differentiated manner. There is a symbiotic quality to their relationships, including the transference, and they seem to hold on to unrealistic hope for change without effort as well as feeling hopeless regarding any change that requires any effort on the part of self or others.

Joseph (1983, p. 295) has examined these issues and notes:

> If our patients are operating largely with early defence mechanisms, the patient who believes he comes in order to be understood, actually comes to use the analyst and analytic situation to maintain his current balance in a myriad of complex and unique ways.
>
> I have been describing patients in whom understanding seems to become unavailable because the part of the ego that might want it is projected into the analyst, and the analyst becomes identified with that part of the self and is then warded off. If the analyst does not watch what is going on in the transference most carefully he may be tempted to prod, as if to suggest that the patient ought to work harder, or be tempted to push superego-ishly to get the patient moving. – If he can really contain this and try to understand why the patient needs to split off and project so much that is potentially valuable in his ego into the analyst, then analysis will go on, as opposed to subtle acting out and moralizing by both patient and analyst: such acting out must lead to a stalemate and most likely to a repetition of what has gone on in the patient's past.

I think this is always a very challenging clinical situation and with the hard-to-reach patient, either paranoid-schizoid or the more primitive pre-depressive patient, this acting out is unavoidable. However, sometimes the analyst can contain, as Joseph recommends, these projections and eventually translate them for the patient.

Yet, even then, some of these patients are so loyal to the use of the death instinct and projective identification as their primary means of defensive organization that it is easy to feel as if one has stepped onto a sinking ship. Slowly but surely it goes down. However, while on this death-boat, the analyst must try to stay the course, act out as little as possible (Feldman 1997, 2009; Steiner 2006, 2011), and continue to offer the patient the life-boat of interpretive understanding.

Betty Joseph (1983, p. 295) notes that these more hard-to-reach patients pose a very special and complicated clinical challenge. She states:

> This type of splitting and projective identification of valuable parts of the ego into the analyst is also seen in very masochistic (patients) – there is a profound split in which the patient remains almost dominated and imprisoned by death instincts, emerging as self-destruction and constant despair, while life instincts, hope, sanity or the desire for progress, are constantly projected into the analyst. In such cases there is little in the patient to balance the pull of the self-destruction, and the patient becomes enthralled and captivated by the exciting self-destructive part of the personality. The patient will unconsciously attempt constantly and actively to undermine the analyst's hope and drag him down into despair. It is very hard for mere

understanding to be anything like as important for these patients as their awful and active masochistic pleasures.

The analyst wrongly assumes that the patient is always seeking and searching for a better life or "mere understanding" as Joseph puts it, one free from fear and guilt and one built on the hope of change, growth, and a life of greater vibrancy. This more optimistic view may be true of those patients who are higher functioning and more stable in their internal psychological make-up. They are anxious about the unknown elements of change and fearful about the outcome of shifting from old to new; but they are still willing to make that risky move and ask us to support them through the stormy, sad, or scary transition. They will resist and retreat at times, but it is clear that they are aware of the benefits of growth and psychic expansion.

However, there are other patients who operate at a much more primitive level and who come to us with the conscious desire to change and grow but unconsciously want us to rebuild their former psychic dwelling, to bring them back to their former psychological status, and to fortify their failing defenses against change and unknown differences.

Feldman and Spillius (1992) discuss the type of patient who comes into treatment because they consciously want to change but once in the treatment process they become unwilling or unable to do so, even though their feeling about analysis and the analyst is usually positive. However, I would add that this generally positive or tolerant attitude towards the analyst is fragile and when the analyst makes interpretations that highlight the patient's reluctance to reflect, change, grow, or allow difference, that attitude can shift, and sometimes shift rather dramatically.

Case material

One patient seemed fairly positive and friendly during the first few sessions of treatment. However, when he realized that I would not literally tell him what to do with his life and show him how to magically stop his lifelong fear of others' judgment, he became very demanding, impatient, and critical. Over the next ten sessions, we were able to explore this by sticking with the moment-to-moment transference situation. However, it was quickly clear that he was probably going to exit the relationship rather soon. He told me he did not trust me, his wife, his friends, or his family and did not think I was interested in helping him.

As the result of my focus on the immediate and total transference (Joseph 1985) and his associations, we were able to discuss and explore his mistrust of his psychotic mother who had been prone to violence when he was young and his sense that no one in his life would accept him or love him unless he could prove that he was special and strong. Yet he often felt weak and scared, and was convinced that he lived in a threatening environment. He felt this way at home, at work, and in the analysis.

In the counter-transference, I found myself in a twofold conflict that is very common with such patients. On one hand, I felt beaten down and put in a situation where I felt there would never be any resolution or change, so I felt like giving up. When he threatened to quit, which was during almost every session, I felt like saying "fine." I did not care and I felt caring was fruitless. It was already a dead and done deal. It was only a matter of time.

On the other hand, I noticed myself trying to work harder than usual making interpretations that mattered and trying my best to convince him that his life could be turned around. I wanted to prove that he could have a better experience of himself and others going ahead if only he hung in there and faced his demons.

He was concrete and I was searching for meaning. He was reluctant and I was encouraging. He was highly anxious and volatile and I was calm and soothing.

So, I noticed this projective identification process in the transference and the intense splitting that took place and pulled me into a variety of feelings that sometimes evolved into enactments. When he finally called me to leave the message I both dreaded and knew was just around the corner, it struck me as one last communication. He said, "I am stopping the treatment. I will not be coming back. I can't afford it." I think that on an unconscious level this patient felt he truly could not emotionally afford to move ahead and give up his current internal status. He was extremely frightened to face what lay ahead and did not think he could afford it, that he could not tolerate it or live through it.

What was this place he had to avoid? I think this was the transition to the shoreline of the depressive position where he would begin to face the more primitive aspects of loss, separation, difference, and uncertainty. He felt more secure wrapped in the defenses of the death instinct where he could ward off difference, the unknown, and the vulnerability of autonomy and change.

The psychological transition and internal conflict these patients face is a disorganized, primitive, and overwhelming version of the depressive position. They are struggling with early life experiences of jarring losses and separations that have left them with a dreadful vision of what should normally be a difficult but soothing and stabilizing developmental move. The depressive position and its foundation of life-instinct experiences is usually a frightening but promising adventure. For these patients, it has become poisoned and perverted and is felt to be a dangerous jungle with some vague rewards to be found but too treacherous a task to risk. So, the patient is shocked when they feel we are offering them this painful journey into the unknown and they often feel betrayed.

When confronted with the splitting of the projective identification system these patients rely on so heavily, the analyst may also end up feeling confused and upset. The mutual effort one hopes for in working with a patient suddenly disappears, if it has ever been there at all, leaving a barren battleground. Suddenly, it seems that there is no effort coming from the patient, and the analyst has to be the spokesperson for the life instincts and the benefits of growth and difference. The only other alternative, in these counter-transference phantasies, is to sink into apathy and despair.

Case material

Jim came to me for help with his anxiety, his chronic depressive feelings, and "the crisis state of my life right now. I can't sleep, I am trying to get on permanent but the paperwork is ridiculous and I have no motivation to do anything." Jim reported growing up "extremely close" to his mother but then his mother died of cancer when he was five years old. He says he "knows this has really defined me." Jim told me his father was very angry and prone to fits of violence and emotional abuse. At the same time, when his father was calm and interested in Jim, Jim says he felt supported by him.

During the course of Jim's one-year analytic treatment, he told me about being molested by a neighbor's older child when Jim was ten years old. He said he trusted this teen and looked up to him. Jim followed him around "like a puppy dog" and felt extremely betrayed and ashamed when this boy told him he had to go along with the molestation "because they were friends." At the same time, Jim felt he was being threatened. He feared "the boy would beat me up if I didn't comply."

As a young adult, Jim was successful in various jobs and got married; but the marriage lasted for only a short time because of how volatile his wife was. Jim later married another woman but left her after two years because of her erratic behavior.

Some five years ago, Jim developed a heart condition that made it impossible for him to do much of anything that required physical exertion. He would become winded if he walked more than a block. When he started seeing me, he had not worked for over a year and was filing for permanent disability. While he did have a severe medical condition that apparently would not get better, I quickly had the feeling that he had limited himself to almost nothing when in fact it sounded as if he was capable of much more. This was the immediate transference and counter-transference situation that I noted. On one hand, I felt as if Jim was working the system and using me as part of that plan; but I also felt that there was something more complicated going on internally, in which Jim no longer saw himself as a viable or capable person worthy of happiness or a vibrant life.

Throughout the treatment, Jim showed an idealizing type of transference in which he was looking for comfort and soothing. He told me he looked forward to the days we met because he "always felt better afterwards. I don't know what it is but I can feel down and troubled and then I come to my appointment and I always walk away feeling better." I noticed that this feeling was something of a one-way street. Jim got something out of the session but I always felt he was passive, concrete, and not really wanting to take ownership of his life. He seemed withholding of his more mature self. In that respect, Jim seemed as if he wanted to have me as a security blanket and a good mother to go to for comfort but did not want to engage with me in more of a mature back and forth.

Jim seemed comfortable in his more stationary state in life instead of finding ways of changing and expanding his life. He wanted help with whatever crisis occurred but did not look beyond those events to a way of being more productive or autonomous. These observations came out of many interactions in which I was curious why he wasn't trying to find a job that suited his physical limitations. Jim always told me he never thought about it and he was sure it was impossible anyway.

I then felt compelled to point out that all he really needed to find was some sort of desk job or cash register position where he mostly sat down. Jim replied in the same pessimistic way when I inquired about why he didn't do any minor exercise when he physically could. When I asked Jim about dating, he also replied in this passive, helpless manner. He told me that "no one would be interested in someone that can't do anything so I have just set that part of my life aside." When I tried to pursue any other areas of exploration, Jim quickly turned the other way. When I tried to examine how he was doing this with me in our therapeutic relationship, Jim ignored this and downplayed it. Of course, this affected me in the complete counter-transference (Waska 2010a, 2010b).

Over the course of our work together, Jim did engage with me to some degree regarding the psychological effects of losing his mother, facing a violent father, suffering the molestation, and ending up with his current physical condition. But, mostly he seemed content to focus on the current crisis state his life always seemed to be in and looked to me for comfort or for concrete answers to external problems without consideration of their internal roots.

During our time together, there seemed to be countless events that happened to Jim, with him as a helpless victim. These were real events but the manner and frequency in which they occurred seemed to show his defined role as victim to external forces and I was the comforting object he could share them with.

So, Jim would have countless headaches that left him feeling unable to get out of bed and make his appointments, including ours. He might have sudden back spasms that took him to the emergency room for the day. He would feel too groggy to get out of bed from the side effects of a new medication. Or, when he went to the dentist, the pain medication for his cavity left him unable to leave the house for two days.

There were sudden arrivals of friends from out of town that Jim had to visit, so he would miss his sessions. His sister had an operation, so he had to go visit her in the hospital. Or, Jim was overwhelmed with paperwork for his disability claims, so he stayed home for days. He was beaten up by thugs in his neighborhood one night, so he ended up in the hospital and recovery took a couple of weeks. Jim fell down the stairs one time and broke his arm, so he had multiple doctors' appointments and had to stay at home to rest for several weeks. There seemed to always be something that prevented him from participating in life, attending his analytic sessions regularly, or from functioning in a fully engaged manner with daily living. Jim seemed to be a constant passive victim to circumstance.

One direction I took was to interpret his possible fear of establishing a consistent bond with me in which he might have to risk sharing with me. Perhaps he did not know whether he could count on me, if I would either disappear, or if I might become a persecutory object. Jim said he understood what I meant but "didn't really feel any of that. I just have things that come up in my life, that's all."

I also interpreted that he might fear becoming more of a full person and facing the world on his own, so he might be finding refuge in remaining "as is." Again, Jim dismissed this but I noticed he was a bit more aggressive in the manner in which he responded. He seemed to put more energy into reminding me of how disabled he was and how impossible it was for him to do anything different. This pulled me into wanting to somehow get him to stop hiding out at home and to begin living a fuller life. When I noticed myself feeling and reacting this way, it helped me see that this was part of a projective identification system in which Jim seemed to discard any life or opportunity into me while he stayed in his passive, inactive shell (Feldman 1992, 1994, 1997; Joseph 1987; Mason 2011; Spillius 1988, 1992). I also interpreted this but Jim told me, "I am fine. I just want to find a way to sleep better and not feel so depressed."

When Jim spoke of feeling depressed, he actually meant that he had been "looking forward to dying" for many years. He said that on any given day, he spent a lot of time looking forward to the day he would die for two reasons. First, he thought of the afterlife as a "wonderful, fantastic experience beyond our wildest dreams." This was not part of any religious belief. Jim also said that he felt life itself was the "most miserable curse possible, a horrible joke played on us." So, it seemed that he idealized the afterlife where he would be given his reward, but for now he had to passively suffer and endure.

I made this interpretation and linked it to possible feelings he had while growing up. Jim thought there could be some validity to him feeling miserable growing up and wishing for a better life, but didn't see how that had much to do with his current situation. I thought of also interpreting his desire to keep me down and lifeless so as to give me a taste of his own childhood and lifelong sense of being immobile; but I thought he would experience that as blaming, so I decided against it.

Over the course of the year with Jim, I noticed two distinct counter-transference states. I ended up feeling either on the side of the death instinct or the life instinct and had the urge to act out one or the other. So, I would feel pulled along in a hopeless, helpless haze, seeing Jim as someone I could never reach and someone who will never amount to much. Or, I would try to rally Jim to join the ranks of the living and make him realize that he too could have a meaningful career, a girlfriend, and a life in which he was more the captain instead of being a passenger on a sinking ship.

However, I think that both of these counter-transference states were the result of his splitting and projection of various internal conflicts he felt completely torn by. I think Jim wanted to avoid the awful pre-depressive world of persecutory loss and the total collapse of confidence in his objects as well as in his own abilities. In addition, Jim seemed to need to create a sadomasochistic stand-off in which he could obtain comfort by projecting the more severe versions of his own struggles with the life-and-death instincts.

Externally, Jim's way of doing that was to be very still and inactive. The result of this was a world that happened to him but one he could manage by not participating and by hiding out. Jim wanted an encouraging, supportive parent who would listen to him, protect him, and comfort him, yet never push him out of the nest into that persecutory pre-depressive world he dreaded.

So, all of my questions and interpretations were experienced as a threatening encouragement to be on his own, lost in the big cruel world where bad things just happen to him. To be more of an active agent meant that he was really on his own without protection and he wanted nothing to do with that. I think part of this was Jim's angry stance of not wanting to grow up until he got all the comforting he deserved. Therefore, he would rebel if pushed to expand, change, or be more responsible for his own thoughts and actions.

Indeed, when I made comments in this direction, Jim became upset and angry. He told me I was "blaming" him for everything that was wrong in his life. Here, I think he was demonstrating the more paranoid-schizoid mode of relating in which he was unable or unwilling to see himself as contributing to anything. Things must be given to him. Things just happen to him. Jim did not want to see that he needs to give to others, to be a part of life, and to make things happen for himself. He was avoiding the depressive position in which there is a back-and-forth, give-and-take participation in the world with sacrifices for others and efforts on one's own behalf.

So, after about two weeks of not coming to his sessions because he had developed a terrible flu which he thought he had caught from waiting in the emergency room the prior week for X-rays of a back problem he was having, Jim arrived and sat down. He told me he thought "things have been going really well and I think I will probably stop coming." I asked for details and Jim told me he felt much happier and "in general I am doing really well." I said I thought he had made progress in different areas but I also wondered about him stopping now. I said there seemed to be ongoing events that happen to him and we hadn't really figured out what that was about. I suggested that perhaps he could learn to have more control over his environment and feel more engaged with life. Again, Jim took this personally and felt I was blaming him.

He said he couldn't believe I was saying he somehow caused all those problems and that he is somehow deliberately creating trouble in his life. I told Jim I was not blaming him but thought he was prone to having life happen around him and that perhaps he was uncomfortable taking a more active role in his life, such as with relationships and with a career. Jim told me that "those things can wait. I will get to them at some point. For now, I just want to relax and enjoy each day since now it is not all about crisis. I came to see you because I was in a crisis and now I am not in one. That is enough for me."

In response to his taking a stronger stance of avoiding further growth or maturity, I found myself starting once again to act out my role of the life instinct. I

said, "You have mentioned still wishing you were dead. So, that might be something worth working a bit more on." Jim said,

> Actually, when I came to see you I wanted to die and leave this shitty world.
> And I couldn't wait to get to the afterlife because it will be so much better.
> If it isn't, then I have endured years of crap for nothing. But, now, I am
> okay living my life and waiting for the afterlife. I still can't wait for the
> afterlife and I will be really happy when I die. But I don't wish to speed up
> my departure date any more.

In the counter-transference, I could feel my resignation creeping in and my
"oh-well" attitude coming into play. In other words, I felt pulled down into more
of a defeated place where I was ready to give up or turn my back on Jim. This
was again the opposite of the other feeling I had of trying to remind him of all
the important work we could still do together and how much better his life could
be.

So, I had to stand on the outside of both of these projective identification-
based states and try to ask myself if I had been doing my best and if I was currently doing all that I could do analytically. Then, I had to ground myself and
simply but painfully accept whatever came next. I had to give up control but not
give up. This was my depressive position conflict in the counter-transference that
I believe Jim could not process in his own mind so he had me travel that road for
him.

We ended the session with the idea that we would meet again to continue discussing this issue. However, not surprisingly, Jim called and told me he was
stopping. He said he was very grateful for all my help, that I had helped him "get
to a better place" and that I "was very understanding and supportive."

Discussion

There are some patients we encounter in psychoanalytic practice who are
extremely resistant to moving towards the more integrated experiences of the
depressive position. They consciously desire help, learning, and change; but,
unconsciously they resist the move towards integration and depressive position
relating. Instead, they try to find balance in their more primitive state of psychic
equilibrium. In the transference, this internal struggle emerges as a constant
reluctance to join the analyst in any psychological shift forward towards emotional transformation and instead the patient favors the more concrete and external factors of daily life as their priority. This creates a therapeutic stand-off with
an either/or and black-or-white type of stance in the transference, the result of
splitting and excessive reliance on projective identification mechanisms.

After a period of this protracted limbo, the clinical climate becomes stale and
still. Consciously, the patient wants change and knowledge; but, in the transference, it seems the patient is avoiding growth, difference, or learning. As a result,

in these more protracted or turbulent cases, the analyst ends up feeling like giving into the patient's prescribed, limited, and strongly defended psychic retreat (Steiner 1993).

Or, the analyst ends up trying too hard to restart the healing process. We start to debate with the patient about the importance of treatment and try to force the patient into health. We find ourselves coming close to saying things like, "Don't you think you could be happier," "Shouldn't you be considering your destructive patterns so that you can change them," or "We still have a way to go." These are red flags that show how in the counter-transference we have become the one who cares, but in an aggressive manner. Suddenly, we are the one who is motivated to find new ways of thinking and feeling while the patient remains complacent, comfortable, and satisfied with the relief of tension or crisis resolution they have found.

So, there are certain patients who seem sadly resigned to existing within a masochistic state of anti-growth and psychological stagnation which is a defensive method of avoiding the threat of depressive loss and uncertainty. They find refuge in paranoid-schizoid ways of relating and fear the consequences of pre-depressive psychic change (Waska 2011a, 2011b).

The transition from paranoid-schizoid to the depressive position involves unfamiliar experiences of powerlessness, guilt, need, and separation (Spillius 1983, 1988; Steiner 1996). Rather than risk these intense conflicts with the life-and-death instincts and the struggle of love, hate, and learning, these difficult or out-of-reach patients tend to use projective identification in the transference to defend themselves. They project their fundamental avoidance of the internal, symbolic, emotional, and relational into the analyst and stay safely focused on the concrete and the external. Thus, in the counter-transference, the analyst can be swept up in acting out the various elements of either of the life-or-death instincts (Waska 2004).

Gradually, for the analytic treatment to have a chance of being successful, the analyst must traverse the same depressive position territory that the patient avoids, slowly interpreting the extreme aspects of both life or death and the conflicts and challenges of living within both (Feldman 2004). In other words, this painful yet rewarding transition may be incorporated into our interpretive efforts and gradually the patient may choose to accept, tolerate, and internalize a bit of it themselves.

Bibliography

Anderson, M. (1999) The Pressure toward Enactment and the Hatred of Reality. *Journal of the American Psychoanalytic Association*, 47: 503–518.

Bell, D. (2011) Bion: The Phenomenon of Loss, in C. Mawson (ed.) *Bion Today*, pp. 81–101, Routledge, London.

Bion, W. (1959) Attacks on Linking. *International Journal of Psychoanalysis*, 40: 308–315.

—— (1962a) A Theory of Thinking. *International Journal of Psychoanalysis*, 43: 306–310.

—— (1962b) *Learning from Experience*, Tavistock, London.

—— (1965) *Transformations*, Karnac, London.

—— (1967) *Second Thoughts*, Heinemann, London.

Britton, R. (1998) *Belief and Imagination: Explorations in Psychoanalysis*, Routledge, London.

Cartwright, D. (2010) *Containing States of Mind: Exploring Bion's Container Model in Psychoanalytic Psychotherapy*, Routledge, London.

Dicks, H. (1967) *Marital Tensions: Clinical Studies toward a Psychological Theory of Interaction*, Routledge, London.

Dougherty, N. (1997) For Better, For Worse: Marital and Family Therapy and the Personality Disorders. *Psychoanalytic Social Work*, 4: 43–59.

Espasa, F. (2002) Considerations on Depressive Conflict and its Different Levels of Intensity: Implications for Technique. *International Journal of Psychoanalysis*, 83: 825–836.

Feldman, M. (1992) Splitting and Projective Identification. In R. Anderson (ed.) *Clinical Lectures on Klein and Bion*, pp. 74–88, Routledge, London.

—— (1994) Projective Identification in Phantasy and Enactment. *Journal of the American Psychoanalytic Association*, 56: 431–453.

—— (1997) Projective Identification: The Analyst's Involvement. *International Journal of Psychoanalysis*, 78: 227–241.

—— (2000) Some Views on the Manifestation of the Death Instinct in Clinical Work. *International Journal of Psychoanalysis*, 81: 53.

—— (2004) Supporting Psychic Change: Betty Joseph. In E. Hargreaves and A. Varchenker (eds) *Pursuit of Psychic Change: The Betty Joseph Workshop*, pp. 20–37, Brunner-Routledge, London.

—— (2009) *Doubt, Conviction, and the Analytic Process*, Routledge, London.

Feldman, M. and Paola, H. (1994) An Investigation into the Psychoanalytic Concept of Envy. *International Journal of Psychoanalysis*, 75: 217–234.

Feldman, M. and Spillius, E. (1992) General Introduction. In *Psychic Equilibrium and Psychic Change: Selected Papers of Betty Joseph*, New Library of Psychoanalysis, Routledge, London.

Gabbard, G. (2004) *Long Term Psychodynamic Psychotherapy: A Basic Text*, American Psychiatric Publishing, London.

Gold, S. (1983) Projective Identification: The Container and Reverie as Concepts in Applied Psychoanalysis. *British Journal of Medical Psychology*, 56: 279.

Grinberg, L. (1962) On a Specific Aspect of Countertransference Due to the Patient's Projective Identification. *International Journal of Psychoanalysis*, 43: 436–440.

—— (1964) Two Kinds of Guilt – Their Relations with Normal and Pathological Aspects of Mourning. *International Journal of Psychoanalysis*, 45: 366–371.

—— (1968) On Acting out and its Role in the Psychoanalytic Process. *International Journal of Psychoanalysis*, 49: 171–178.

—— (1977) An Approach to the Understanding of Borderline Disorders. In P. Hartocollis (ed.) *Borderline Personality Disorders: The Concept, the Syndrome, the Patient*, pp. 123–141, International Universities Press, New York.

—— (1990) *The Goals of Psychoanalysis: Identification, Identity, and Supervision*, Karnac, London.

Grotstein, J. (1994) Projective Identification Reappraised – Part I: Projective Identification, Introjective Identification, the Transference/Countertransference Neurosis/Psychosis, and their Consummate Expression in the Crucifixion, the Pieta, and "Therapeutic Exorcism." *Contemporary Psychoanalysis*, 30: 708–746.

—— (2009) *But at the Same Time on a Different Level: Psychoanalytic Theory and Technique in the Kleinian/Bionian Mode*, Vol. 1, Karnac, London.

Hargreaves, E. and Varchenker, A. (2004) *In Pursuit of Psychic Change: The Betty Joseph Workshop*, Routledge, London.

Hinshelwood, R. (1989) *A Dictionary of Kleinian Thought*, Jason Aronson, New York.

—— (1999) Countertransference. *International Journal of Psychoanalysis*, 80(4): 797–818.

—— (2004) Contrasting Clinical Techniques: A British Kleinian, Contemporary Freudian and Latin American Kleinian Discuss Clinical Material. *International Journal of Psychoanalysis*, 85(5): 1257–1260.

Joseph, B. (1978) Different Types of Anxiety and Their Handling in the Analytic Situation. *International Journal of Psychoanalysis*, 59: 223–227.

—— (1982) Addiction to Near-Death. *International Journal of Psychoanalysis*, 63: 449–456.

—— (1983) On Understanding and not Understanding: Some Technical Issues. *International Journal of Psychoanalysis*, 64: 291–298.

—— (1985) Transference: The Total Situation. *International Journal of Psychoanalysis*, 66: 447–454.

—— (1987) Projective Identification: Clinical Aspects. In J. Sandler (ed.) *Projection, Identification, Projective Identification*, pp. 65–76, International Universities Press, Madison, CT.

—— (1988) Object Relations in Clinical Practice. *Psychoanalytic Quarterly*, 57: 626–642.

—— (1989) *Psychic Equilibrium and Psychic Change: Selected Papers of Betty Joseph*, edited by M. Feldman and E. B. Spillius, New Library of Psychoanalysis, Tavistock/Routledge, London and New York.

—— (1997) *The Pursuit of Insight and Psychic Change: Conference on Psychic Structure and Psychic Change*, University College, London.

Kavaler-Adler, S. (2004) Anatomy of Regret: A Developmental View of the Depressive Position and a Critical Turn Toward Love and Creativity in the Transforming Schizoid Personality. *American Journal of Psychoanalysis*, 64: 39–76.

Kernberg, O. (2011) Limitations to the Capacity to Love. *International Journal of Psychoanalysis*, 92(6): 1501–1515.

Klein, M. (1935) A Contribution to the Psychogenesis of Manic-Depressive States, The Writings of Melanie Klein, in Love, Guilt, and Reparation and Other Works 1921–1945. In *The Writings of Melanie Klein*, Vol. 1, p. 262, Free Press, London.

—— (1940) Mourning and its Relation to Manic-Depressive States. *International Journal of Psychoanalysis*, 21: 125–153.

—— (1946) Notes on Some Schizoid Mechanisms. *International Journal of Psychoanalysis*, 27: 99–110.

Mason, A. (2011) Projective Identification. In E. Spillius and E. O'Shaughannesy (eds) *Projective Identification: The Fate of a Concept*, pp. 301–320, Routledge, London.

Mawson, C. (2011) Introduction: Bion Today – Thinking in the Field. In C. Mawson (ed.) *Bion Today*, Routledge, London.

Paniagua, C. (2003) Problems with the Concept Interpretation. *International Journal of Psychoanalysis*, 84: 1105–1123.

Pao, P. (1977) On the Formation of Schizophrenic Symptoms. *International Journal of Psychoanalysis*, 58: 389–401.

Perelbberg, J. (2009) On Becoming a Psychoanalyst. *Psychoanalytic Inquiry*, 29, 247–263.

Quinodoz, J. (1996) The Sense Of Solitude In The Psychoanalytic Encounter. *International Journal of Psychoanalysis* 77: 481–496.

Racker, H. (1953) A Contribution to the Problem of Countertransference. *International Journal of Psychoanalysis*, 34: 313–324.

—— (1957) The Meanings and Uses of Countertransference. *Psychoanalytic Quarterly*, 26: 303–357.

Riesenberg, M. (1990) As If: The Phenomenon of Not Learning. *International Journal of Psychoanalysis*, 73: 385–392.

Riviere, J. (1936) A Contribution to the Analysis of the Negative Therapeutic Reaction. *International Journal of Psychoanalysis*, 17: 304–320.

Rosenfeld, H. (1964) On the Psychopathology of Narcissism: A Clinical Approach. *International Journal of Psychoanalysis*, 45: 332–337.

—— (1971) A Clinical Approach to the Psychoanalytic Theory of the Life and Death Instincts: An Investigation Into the Aggressive Aspects of Narcissism. *International Journal of Psychoanalysis*, 52: 169–178.

—— (1979) Difficulties in the Psychoanalysis of Borderline Patients. In J. LeBoit and A. Capponi (eds) *Advances in Psychotherapy of the Borderline Patient*, pp. 203–204, Jason Aronson, New York.

—— (1983) Primitive Object Relations and Mechanisms. *International Journal of Psychoanalysis*, 64: 261–267.

—— (1987) *Impasse and Interpretation: Therapeutic and Anti-Therapeutic Factors in the Psychoanalytic Treatment of Psychotic, Borderline, and Neurotic Patients.* New Library of Psychoanalysis, Vol. 1, Tavistock, London.

Roth, P. (1994) Being True to a False Object: A View of Identification. *Psychoanalytic Quarterly*, 14: 393–405.

Rubin, M. (2004) The Fictive Object and Disordered Attachments. *Contemporary Psychoanalysis*, 40: 175–195.

Ruggiero, I. (2012) The Unreachable Ego. *International Journal of Psychoanalysis*, 93(3): 341–362.

Sander, F. (2004) Psychoanalytic Couples Therapy: Classical Style. *Psychoanalytic Inquiry*, 24: 373–386.

Sandler, J. (1976) Countertransference and Role-Responsiveness. *International Review of Psycho-Analysis*, 3: 43–47.

Schafer, R. (1994) The Contemporary Kleinians of London. *Psychoanalytic Quarterly*, 63: 409–432.

—— (2002) Experiencing Termination: Authentic and False Depressive Positions, Psychoanalytic Psychology, 19: 235–253

Segal, H. (1977) Psychoanalytic Dialogue: Kleinian Theory Today. *Journal of the American Psychoanalytic Association*, 25: 363–370.

—— (1981) *The Work of Hanna Segal: A Kleinian Approach to Clinical Practice*, Jason Aronson, New York.

—— (1987) Silence is the Real Crime. *Annual Review of Psychoanalysis*, 14: 3–12.

—— (1993) On the Clinical Usefulness of the Concept of Death Instinct. *International Journal of Psychoanalysis*, 74: 55–61.

—— (1997) Some Implications of Melanie Klein's Work: Emergence from Narcissism. In J. Steiner (ed.) *Psychoanalysis, Literature, and War*, pp. 75–85, Routledge, London.

Segal, H. and Britton, R. (1981) Interpretation and Primitive Psychic Processes: A Kleinian View. *Psychoanalyst Inquiry*, 1: 267–277.

Siegel, J. (1998) Defensive Splitting in Couples. *Journal of Clinical Psychoanalysis*, 7: 305–327.

—— (2004) Identifications as a Focal Point in Couples Therapy. *Psychoanalytic Inquiry*, 24: 406–419.

Sodre, I. (2004) Who's Who: Notes on Pathological Identification. In E. Hargreaves and A. Varchenker (eds) *In Pursuit of Psychic Change: The Betty Joseph Workshop*, pp. 53–68, Routledge, London.

Spillius, E. (1983) Some Developments from the Work of Melanie Klein. *International Journal of Psychoanalysis*, 64: 321–332.

—— (1988) *Melanie Klein Today. Developments in Theory and Practice*, Vol. I: *Mainly Theory*, edited by E. B. Spillius, New Library of Psychoanalysis, Routledge, London and New York.

—— (1992) Clinical Experiences of Projective Identification. In R. Anderson (ed.) *Clinical Lectures on Klein and Bion*, pp. 59–73, Routledge, London.

Spillius, E. and Feldman, M. (1989) *Psychic Equilibrium and Psychic Change: Selected Papers of Betty Joseph*, The New Library of Psychoanalysis, edited by M. Feldman and E. B. Spillius, Vol. 9, Tavistock/Routledge, London and New York.

Spillius, E., Milton, J., Garvey, P., Couve, C. and Steiner, D. (2011) *The New Dictionary of Kleinian Thought*, Routledge, London.

Steiner, J. (1979) The Border Between the Paranoid-Schizoid and the Depressive Positions in the Borderline Patient. *British Journal of Medical Psychology*, 52, 285–391.

—— (1987) The Interplay Between Pathological Organizations and the Paranoid-Schizoid and Depressive Positions. *International Journal of Psychoanalysis*, 68: 69–80.

—— (1990) Pathological Organizations as Obstacles to Mourning: The Role of Unbearable Guilt. *International Journal of Psychoanalysis*, 71: 87–94.

—— (1992) The Equilibrium Between the Paranoid and the Depressive Position. In R. Anderson (ed.) *Clinical Lectures on Klein and Bion*, pp. 46–58, Routledge, London.

—— (1993) *Psychic Retreats: Pathological Organizations in Psychotic, Neurotic, and Borderline Patients*, New Library of Psychoanalysis, Vol. 19, Routledge, London and New York.

—— (1996) The Aim of Psychoanalysis in Theory and in Practice. *International Journal of Psychoanalysis*, 77: 1073–1083.

—— (2000) Containment, Enactment and Communication. *International Journal of Psychoanalysis*, 81: 245–255.

—— (2004) Gaze, Dominance and Humiliation in the Schreber Case. *International Journal of Psychoanalysis*, 85(2): 269–284.

—— (2006) Interpretive Enactments and the Analytic Setting. *International Journal of Psychoanalysis*, 87(2): 315–320.

—— (2008) The Repetition Compulsion, Envy, and the Death Instinct. In P. Roth and A. Lemma (eds) *Envy and Gratitude Revisited*, p. 137, Karnac, London.

—— (2011) *Seeing and Being Seen: Emerging From a Psychic Retreat*, Routledge, London.

Steiner, R. (1989) Review of *Some Observations on Projection, Identification, Projective Identification*, Edited by Joseph Sandler, Karnac Books, London, 1988. *International Journal of Psychoanalysis*, 70: 727–735.

Sweet, A. (2010) Paranoia and Psychotic Process: Some Clinical Applications of Projective Identification in Psychoanalytic Psychotherapy. *American Journal of Psychotherapy*, 64(4): 339–358.

Waska, R. (2002) *Primitive Experiences of Loss: Working with the Paranoid-Schizoid Patient*, Karnac, London.

—— (2004) *Projective Identification: The Kleinian Interpretation*, Brunner/Routledge, London.

—— (2005) *Real People, Real Problems, Real Solutions: The Kleinian Approach to Difficult Patients*, Brunner/Routledge, London.

—— (2006) *The Danger of Change: The Kleinian Approach with Patients who Experience Progress as Trauma*, Brunner/Routledge, London.

—— (2007) *The Concept of Analytic Contact: A Kleinian Approach to Reaching the Hard to Reach Patient*, Brunner/Routledge, London.

—— (2010a) *Treating Severe Depressive and Persecutory Anxieties States: Using Analytic Contact to Transform the Unbearable*, Karnac, London.

—— (2010b) *Love, Hate, and Knowledge: The Kleinian Method of Analytic Contact and the Future of Psychoanalysis*, Karnac, London.

—— (2010c) *Selected Theoretical and Clinical Issues in Psychoanalytic Psychotherapy: A Modern Kleinian Approach to Analytic Contact*, Novoscience, New York.

—— (2010d) *The Modern Kleinian Approach to Psychoanalysis: Clinical Illustrations*, Jason Aronson, New York.

—— (2011a) *Moments of Uncertainty in Psychoanalytic Practice: Interpreting Within the Matrix of Projective Identification, Counter-Transference, and Enactment*, Columbia University Press, Columbia, OH.

—— (2011b) *The Total Transference and the Complete Counter-Transference: The Kleinian Psychoanalytic Approach with More Disturbed Patients*, Jason Aronson, New York.

—— (2012) *Success and Failure in Psychoanalysis: Klein in the Trenches*, Rodopi Press, New York.

—— (2013) *A Practical Casebook of Time-Limited Psychoanalytic Work: A Modern Kleinian Approach*, Routledge, London.

Williams, G. (2013) No Entry: An Invitation to Intrude, or Both? *International Journal of Psychoanalysis*, 94(4): 684–713.

Index

abandoned 54, 58–9, 84, 113–14, 128
abandonment 4, 20, 27, 118, 134, 146
addictive 85; character profiles 19;
    relational profiles 83
aggressive 59, 66; anxiety 92; attack 20,
    39, 125, 140; defense 88, 109; demand
    118; less 141; manner 18, 157; more
    154; motivation 45, 108; quests 20, 39;
    return of projections 32; transference
    effort 98, 139
analyst 1, 3, 5, 10, 61, 83, 87, 96, 98, 120,
    133, 156; acting out 139; attacked 135;
    authority figures 123; balanced moments
    82; confused and upset 151; counter-
    transference 56, 58, 86, 134, 137,
    147–8; difficult patients 138, 142–4;
    enactments 48; engagement with the
    pathological organizations 89–90, 93;
    experience of termination 54;
    exploration of unconscious phantasies
    97; initial phase difficulties 23;
    interested 68; internalize 121;
    interpersonal pressures on 18, 38;
    interpreting 19, 32, 40, 114; limited 88;
    limit setting 94–5; manipulation 31,
    56–7, 59– 60, 76–7; parental container
    122; perceived threat 109; primary
    counter-transference states 4; pushed to
    the limits 2; rejection of 128; role in the
    patient's mind 59; used by patients
    149–50, 157; validating patient's fears
    44; weight of projections 49, 55;
    working on static chaos 108
analytic treatment 1–2, 24, 35, 40, 54, 56,
    63, 92, 107, 136, 152, 157; see also
    psychoanalytic treatment
anger 12, 14–15, 18, 37, 39, 64, 66, 68, 77,
    91–2, 114, 118, 137–8; camouflaged 142

annihilation 19–20, 83, 85, 108
anxieties 1–2, 4, 11, 18, 26, 34–5, 47, 62,
    65, 85–6, 98, 101, 105–7, 115, 128, 138,
    144, 146, 152; aggressive 92;
    annihilation 85; anti-anxiety medication
    23; attacks 12; constant 27, 91; core
    feelings 72; depressive 10, 19, 83–5,
    133, 142, 145; depressive position 32;
    intense 33, 57, 68, 70; about knowing
    20, 39; mutual 95; near-psychotic 85;
    paranoid and depressive 31, 44, 82–3,
    114; paranoid-schizoid 84, 87, 96,
    138–9, 141; persecutory 98; personal
    99; physical experiences 21; primary 17,
    58, 84, 113; projective-based 108;
    protection from 143; reduction 56–7, 63;
    relief from 109, 122, 136; separation 20;
    sharing 25; state 30; transference 44;
    unbearable 19, 40, 114
avoid 92, 127, 134, 146, 151; being in
    touch with self 70; breakdown 128;
    challenge 91; depressive pain 21, 116,
    154; internal fragmentation 142;
    knowledge 18; phantasies 85;
    unbearable feelings 17, 19, 83, 120
avoidance 48, 69; of change 107; of
    individuation 54; mutual 83; of personal
    need 134; projection of 157

Bell, D. 32, 116
Bion, W. 9, 18, 20, 31, 38, 40, 48, 56, 69,
    76, 81, 109, 114, 122
boyfriend 36, 49–50, 52; driven away 127;
    ex 103; new 65; old 101

Cartwright, D. 68, 87, 114, 116
challenges 2, 4, 21, 33, 39, 66, 72, 91,
    115, 157; clinical 149; narcissistic 93;

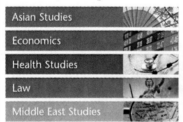